FOLKTALES FROM IRAQ

FOLKTALES FROM IRAQ

Edited and translated by
C. G. CAMPBELL

Illustrated by
John Buckland Wright

PENN

University of Pennsylvania Press
Philadelphia

Originally published 1949 by Lindsay Drummond
Printed in the United States of America on acid-free paper

10 9 8 7 6 5 4 3 2 1

Published 2005 by
University of Pennsylvania Press
Philadelphia, Pennsylvania 19104-4011

Library of Congress Cataloging-in-Publication Data

Campbell, C. G. (Charles Grimshaw).
  Folktales from Iraq / a collection of the stories told by the Arab
tribes of the Lower Euphrates translated and set down by C. G.
Campbell and illustrated by John Buckland Wright
    p. cm.
  Includes bibliographical references
  ISBN 0-8122-1913-9 (pbk. : alk. paper)
  Originally published: Tales from the Arab tribes. London :
Lindsay Drummond, 1949.
  1. Arabs—Iraq—Folklore. 2. Tales—Iraq. I. Title. II. Buckland
Wright, John, 1897–1954.
GR295.I7 C35 2005
398.2'09567—dc22   2005042174

CONTENTS

CONTENTS

The Muntafiq Revisited

FOLKTALES FROM IRAQ

PREFACE

IN Victorian days it was customary to preface a translated work with an apology for imperfections in the translation. I would say that I am not an interpreter such as those of the United Nations, who can listen to a long speech in one language and who afterwards can render it accurately and with perfect memory in another language. I am also conscious that these stories when told with a wealth of gesture and expression of face and voice were things of vivid beauty like rare butterflies, and in reducing them to paper it is as if they have been killed and pinned in a collector's cabinet.

These stories belong to the great Shia tribes of Southern Iraq. I first came into contact with these tribes when, coming over from the Western Desert in the winter of 1942, I halted on the road near Ur, and engaged a couple of likely-looking tribesmen to show me what local shooting there was, and to act as guides. The next day we drove far into the desert after bustard, and coming over a rise in the ground we saw before us a group of long, low, black tents; in my ignorance I turned to my two guides and asked them what the tribe of these bedouin was. Their faces registered horror and surprise, and they said: 'Those are not bedouin; they are Arabs.' Not having been previously aware of this distinction, I asked them how they told the difference between bedouin and Arab. They replied: 'We thought because you speak Arabic you would know the difference.' They went on to point out large numbers of sheep dotted around the horizon and they explained that had there been a large number of camels with a few sheep, then bedouin would have been indicated. Instead there was a large number of sheep with a few camels, indicating Arabs. They had to go on to explain that by Arabs they meant the great landowning Shia tribes, who are in the main cultivators of rice, dates, barley and a variety of other crops, but they send out their sheep on long treks through the desert in charge of some of their families in search of grass.

Most of the Arab tribes are dwellers in houses or clean, cool huts made of reed matting, which allows for a constant current of air through the hut, and prevents the temperature from rising to that of an oven in the hot sun, like a house. Many of these stories were told in a large guest house or tent pitched amongst the houses, with a background of sound varying from that of the cooking of a meal of several roast sheep to the powerful thump, thump, thump, of the great pumps. These pumps deserve mention, since they are often a tribe's principal pride and source of wealth. At one place I was surprised to hear that a boy's name was Rustam, since this name is more common amongst Persians and Kurds than amongst Arabs, but it was explained to me that he was named after the pump, and I understood when I saw the name Rustom stamped on an iron plate on the great cylinder.

The Arab tribes have a great military history of which they are justly proud. It is long and somewhat complicated, and to give in full the history of a single tribe as told by the sheikhs would fill a book greater in size than this. I will, however, give a précis of the history of that great group of tribes which were known as the Muntafiq.

The Muntafiq was a confederation of the Shia tribes living around the Gharraf River and around what is now the town of Nasiriya, drawn together for the purpose of opposing the Turks by Saadun of the Sunni family of Es Shabib, who became the founder of the house of Saadun. The tribes of the Muntafiq used to raid the Turks in the Basra area and harry their convoys on the road to Baghdad. However, in 1775 a new threat developed in South Iraq in the form of a Persian advance on Basra, and the Saadun leaders of the Muntafiq apparently decided that the Turks were the lesser evil, for they sent a force of their cavalry to assist them and stationed it at the ancient village of Zobeir.

Throughout the siege of the city the Muntafiq cavalry remained at Zobeir, which is about ten miles from Basra and separated from it by a salt plain liable to flood. The tribal horse, under Sheikh Abdulla es Saadun and Sheikh Thamir es Saadun, could not have been of much assistance to the garrison of the city, for the fighting was taking place in the belt of palm trees interspersed by numerous creeks which surrounds the town on all but one side; and the Persian infantry were assisted by that redoubtable tribe of watermen, the Kaab, who were particularly valuable in the area of marsh which used to extend from what in the last war was the military camp area of Makina to what is now the modern port of Maqil. It appears to have been a major error that the Muntafiq did not bring their footmen and boats down to assist in the defence of Basra, for the country was quite unsuited to cavalry; but it must be remembered that the Muntafiq could only have been lukewarm allies of the Turks, whom they had been fighting so recently.

Basra surrendered to the Persians in the spring of 1776,

4

after a defence in which the Turkish garrison did not distinguish themselves. The Muntafiq force, however, remained at Zobeir, from where they controlled all exits from Basra to the desert, and the Euphrates route to Baghdad. It soon became apparent to Ali Muhammed, the Persian commander, that a port without a hinterland is a doubtful acquisition, but he took no measures against the Muntafiq tribesmen until 1778, when sheer boredom and the necessity of tending to their crops had reduced the Muntafiq force at Zobeir to practically nothing. Then, after a surprise attack, the village fell easily to the Persians, and Ali Muhammed ordered the Muntafiq garrison to be put to the sword.

The fury of the great tribes of the Muntafiq knew no bounds when they heard the news of the loss of Zobeir, involving as it did the rape and death of some Muntafiq women. Hawasing, or the singing of war songs accomanied by war dances, inaugurated a general rising of the whole Muntafiq confederation, the much dreaded 'Hamrat el Muntafiq'. Sheikh Thamir es Saadun took command of the Muntafiq forces, and a large horsed contingent marched down on Basra over the desert, while the tribal boats came down over the Hammar lake, and the footmen marched down the banks of the Euphrates River and the lake itself. Some ten thousand Persians marched out of Basra under Ali Muhammed to do battle, and the Persians also put on the river a flotilla of some twenty Basra jalbuts on which they had mounted guns and which had crews impressed from Basra itself. The redoubtable Kaab were absent from their order of battle.

The Persians seem to have learnt many false lessons in their campaign against Basra, and the most fatal of these was their belief that the Muntafiq tribes were desert

5

fighters unable to manoeuvre in the palm belts and marshes. Thus, when their advanced guard cavalry gained contact with the Muntafiq horse in the desert Ali Muhammed successfully manoeuvred his force to drive them into the marshes and into what appeared to be a trap, an area surrounded on all but the entrance side by marsh or by bends of the river. The main Persian force entered this area to complete the destruction of the trapped tribesmen, but soon realised that the marshes were swarming with Muntafiq footmen.While the river held only tribal boats, there was no sign of the Persian flotilla, which, some say, had already been destroyed. When they attempted to retreat from this death-trap, the Persians found their escape blocked by more mounted tribesmen from the desert. Thamir es Saadun is said to have raised his sword and ordered a general massacre of the Persian force, a departure from the tribes' usual custom of taking prisoners, in revenge for the atrocities at Zobeir. Ali Muhammed was amongst the slain, and it is said that only three men escaped alive.

As a direct result of this disaster, in which they lost a major part of their force, the Persians evacuated Basra in the following year. This victory over the Persians was the Muntafiq's greatest success, but it also contained the seeds of the final dissolution of the Confederation, since the Shia tribes had been drawn together under Sunni leadership for the common purpose of opposing the Turks. After this battle the policy of the paramount sheikhs, the Saaduns, became more and more pro-Turkish, and by the middle of the nineteenth century we find that the paramount sheikh had almost invariably the title of Pasha, and was supported by the Turks in his rule of the Muntafiq. The tribal army now underwent a change: the great

6

Shia tribes sent less and less of their men to rally to the Muntafiq standard, and the tribal cavalry consisted of paid retainers of the ruling house. There were, it is true, occasional differences between the Saaduns and the Turks, as when the powerful Saadun Pasha was at loggerheads with the Wali of Basra.

The Confederation is a thing of the past, and its Shia tribesmen now owe loyalty only to their own tribal sheikhs, and above them to the Government of Iraq. It is touching to find in some remote reed hut carefully tended pictures of King Feisal and of His Royal Highness the Regent. The tribes had their greatest glory in the days when the country was under foreign domination, when they were the rallying-points of the resistance which prevented the absorption of Iraq into either Turkey or Persia. In a democratic state the position of the tribes is less clear. There is much that is fine in tribal life and worth preserving at all costs, and a tribal loyalty need not necessarily interfere with modern progress. For example, numbers of tribesmen from all over Iraq now live in the capital, working in various jobs, as artisans and labourers, lawyers, doctors and engineers. In this growing State a boy may be born in a tribal reed hut, and if intelligent finish up as a doctor in Baghdad. All these emigrants from the tribes maintain close contact with their tribes, usually by way of entertaining tribesmen on their visits to the city. When a sheikh makes a levy, for some purpose, of a dirhem from the head of every family in his tribe, the emigrants are the first to send in their money: though they may be wealthy doctors driving American saloon cars, they send in the exact dirhem along with the labourers and artisans. To send more would savour of ostentation.

Life in the tribes is changing year by year. The pumping

7

engines owned by every tribe send thousands of tons of the brown waters of the Euphrates down the irrigation channels to make the land fertile and green. Education is spreading to the tribes, and an increasing number of tribesmen hold jobs of every sort in the railways, the port, and the oil companies. Many tribesmen from the Euphrates drove trucks on the great Aid to Russia route through Persia during the war. Others could be found serving the Allied war effort as far apart as Masira at the end of the Persian Gulf and Haifa.

With this development going on all around him, it is not surprising that the amusements of the tribesman are changing. Whereas before he had to amuse himself by listening to stories told by amateur but skilled storytellers, he can now pass the evening listening to a wireless set driven off the battery of his sheikh's or his sirkal's saloon car, or better still, he can jump a bus or lorry into the nearest village and watch an Egyptian, Indian, or American film. In this atmosphere it is not surprising that the stories are dying out, and now only a few of the older men know them. These stories fulfilled a need in the days in which the tribes were in constant conflict with the Turkish Government, and in which facilities for written Arabic literature did not exist. Now, in more prosperous times, they must die out. I would stress that the stories were never considered as belonging to any great school of Arabic literature—they were simple little things, either originated by the tribesmen themselves or adapted from some more ancient story, and their intention was merely to evoke a smile on an arduous march, or to help pass a cold desert night; and so they must be judged.

To those who want the real beauty of a precise language, I say that this can be found in written classical Arabic, but I warn them that Arabic is an Everest of languages, not to be stormed by some carefree explorer bent on a year or so of study. Seven years of steady plodding may bring the explorer to the snowline, but the icy peaks still tower above him in all their clear beauty, as they have stood for over two thousand years, nor are their slopes safe for any but Arab feet to tread. In the words of Ibn ed Dahhan they may well say:

'Do not think that you will be a poet such as we, for though the hen is feathered, it does not fly.'

THE STORY OF HAJJI ALI, THE

GREAT SULTAN, AND HIS SON,
THE AMIR KHEYYUN

And this story was written on a night of rain and flood, and the storyteller was Hamud.

NOW there was a Sultan from amongst the Sultans who ruled Iraq before the days of the Ottomans, and his name was Hajji Ali. And this Sultan had only one son, the Amir Kheyyun, who was a youth of twenty years, so handsome of the face that when he passed through the city the people would come out and throng the streets, and so dense were the crowds that not even a flea could pass through the town. And the Amir Kheyyun was famous in battle, for he commanded the armies of the Sultan, and he challenged the enemies of the Sultan his father to single combat, and used to kill them in front of their armies. And he obeyed the commands of the Sultan his father in everything, for this is the custom of the Arabs.

So one day the Sultan, Hajji Ali, sent for his son, Kheyyun, and he said: In this world only one thing is certain and only one thing is known, and that is that death comes to every man, nor can a single man escape from it. And the time is not long nor shall many years pass before you are Sultan of this land in my place, but (may it be far from you) when you are dead who shall replace you? Therefore it is now suitable that you take a wife. But Kheyyun, the obedient son, refused the command of his father, nor did he heed his words. And he said: I have studied the matter, and I have read every book concerning women, which has been written by every wise man and philosopher of Iraq, of Persia, of India, of China and of Rome, and I have come to the conclusion that women are evil, and they are witches, nor is there truth and goodness in them. Therefore, how can a man take one of them for a wife?

And the Sultan thought: This is only the foolishness of youth. I will command my son to marry in the presence of my ministers, my advisers, and my troops, then, through shame, he cannot disobey me. And he summoned his court, his ministers, and his troops, and he sent for the sheikhs and leading men of the country, and the palace was thronged with a great crowd, and he sent for his son, the Amir Kheyyun.

And the Sultan spoke and said: It is long since we have had celebrations and rejoicing as is fitting in a great city on the occasion of a royal marriage or the birth of an heir to the throne. I therefore command and order the Minister of Finance to produce a sum of one hundred thousand dirhems, and that each of the sheikhs of the tribes shall bring one thousand Syrian sheep, and each of the great merchants shall bring one thousand bags of the finest rice of Amara and of El Huweiza, and the Governor of Basra shall bring one thousand boatloads of the sweetest dates in Basra, and the Maadan shall bring milk, and the people of Mosul shall bring honey, and of Baquba, fruit, and from each town and village shall come the fruits and crops and vegetables of that village. And for every day of the first month of the new year one thousand sheep shall be killed and roasted and stuffed with walnuts and almonds, nor shall any man in the city go hungry, and the travellers and the people of the desert shall also be satisfied, for in that auspicious month will be celebrated the wedding of my son, the Amir Kheyyun, the beloved.

And the Amir Kheyyun stood up in front of his father, and he said: No. Then the faces of the great sheikhs and the great merchants and the captains of ships and the commanders of troops and the learned men became red with shame, for amongst the Arabs it is not fitting that a son speak in front of his father and into his father's face.

And the Sultan became white with rage, and he ordered: Imprison him.

Then the guards and the officers of the Sultan seized the Amir and they took him away to the jail. And let it be known to you that the jail to which they took the Amir is unlike the jail with which you are acquainted, namely, that jail which lies at the Zobeir Gate of Basra City. It was also unlike the camps surrounded by wire in which the English keep the Germans at Shuaiba. For this prison was one especially for princes and the highest in the land. It was like a palace, and the walls were of marble and rare stones, and anything that a man could desire was available. Only the guards at the gate forbade the Amir Kheyyun to go out from it.

Now it happened one day that a fisherman went to the river in the morning, and at the rising of the sun he threw his net into the water and drew it back. In that net was a fish of gold, the like of which had never been seen before throughout the whole land of Iraq. And the fisherman talked with his comrades and said: I will take this fish to the Amir who is in the prison, for it may make him happy and it may bring him fortune. And he took the fish and put it in a bowl of water and took it to the prison and gave it to the Amir. And the Amir was happy for he had never before seen such a fish.

So the Amir made a pool for that fish, of which the sides were of gold and silver, and he sat by the pool and watched the beauty of the fish. And he remained for three hours appreciating its beauty. For the whole three hours the fish did not stand or stop, but it went at speed from one end of the pool to the other. And the Amir thought: Why does the fish not stop? Why does it dash about? It is a tragedy for it. Like me it is a prisoner. It needs the river.

13

And the Amir took that fish and threw it in the river. Now that fish was of the tribe of Adam, and it was really a girl, for you know that the fish of gold are really of the tribe of men, though they have taken the disguise of fish, and are skilled in magic and unusual things. And as the Amir threw the fish into the river he said: May God leave you with your lover and may he leave me with a lover.

Now when the fish girl landed in the water she swam off to her lover, to a cave beneath the waters of the Tigris, and he asked her: Where have you been and why have you delayed your coming? And she replied: I was taken in a net, and given to the Amir, but he returned me to the water and he said, Go to your lover.

But when the Amir had told his father the Sultan that all girls were witches and evil creatures he was lying, nor did he fully state the truth, for one girl, a princess in a neighbouring country, he thought not evil but good, and his blood was hot with love for her, but he concealed this from his father, knowing that the Sultan wished to marry him to his cousin, that her wealth might not go from Iraq.

And the lover of the fish girl was aware of these affairs, for of such are the magicians. And he thought: I must reward the Amir who gave me back my beloved. And he took on the shape of a derwish, and went to the prison, and saluted the Amir. And he said: You desire to take Aliya bint Rejab. When the Amir saw that his desire was known to the derwish he became as white as milk, and he was astonished, and he implored help from the derwish, saying: O master of miracles, help me get my beloved. And the Amir and the derwish mounted on horses and left the prison, nor did the guards become aware of their departure. They rode to the palace of the girl Aliya. And

15

they entered the palace like cats, in the second half of the night, and the alarm was not raised. And the Amir went into the room of the girl Aliya. The night was hot and she had cast off her clothes. And when the Amir saw the beauty of her body he was amazed, and he was near to fainting with wonder. But he covered the girl Aliya and took her to the horses, and they rode into the desert. And in the morning they halted and she cooked for them food.

When they had eaten of meat and rice and dates and lebn the derwish spoke to the Amir and said: It is written that we must divide this girl between us and each have his share of her, for if two are partners in labour they must share the achievement. And the Amir said: This suggestion is unsuitable, nor can it happen thus. And the girl heard and was amazed at the words of the derwish. But the derwish insisted and said: A division is written as the fate of this girl, and I have no power to alter it. The Amir thought: This derwish is one of the princes of magicians, and he has befriended me. So he said: If it is thus, then it shall be done according to your wishes, but how shall we divide her, up and down, or across? And the derwish replied: Up and down, for then each of us shall have a beautiful eye and a breast and an arm and a leg and it will be even between us, and neither shall have an advantage. The girl Aliya heard these words and became afraid. She cast herself at the derwish's feet and cried: O my masters, cast lots between yourselves as to which is to have me, but do not divide me. But the derwish said: It is necessary. And he drew his sword and waved it over the girl and was about to strike, and the Amir Kheyyun covered his eyes from the spectacle. But at that very moment the girl's mouth opened and the head of a snake appeared from it. And the derwish cried: Come out, Zeboshun,

Come out, Zeboshun. And the snake came out and it was twenty feet long and green of skin, and it went over the desert with the speed of a horse. The derwish turned to the Amir and said: I have frightened the snake from her, for it was in her and she knew it not. For this snake was of a breed which enters girls without their knowledge, and its pleasure lies in the torment of men, for it waits for the girl to marry, then it causes her to be angry and nag her man, and her words become as the very venom of the snake, and there is no means of extracting the snake, unless you see its face and know its name and gain power over it.

The Amir was grateful and thanked the derwish, and the derwish said: The girl is yours and I wish you enjoyment in her, and peace be on you and in God's hands. So the Amir took the girl and married her and went to his father's palace. The servants and slaves cried: Your father is stricken with grief for you. And the Amir went to his father the Sultan Hajji Ali and said: Peace on you, O my father, I have taken a wife in accordance with your wishes. And the Sultan became glad and rejoiced and he made his son reign in his place, and he was a wise and just ruler, and had many sons, beautiful as moons.

A STORY CONCERNING THE

IGNORANCE OF SLAVES

One day we were halted on the road to Fao. A Negro passed, a slave, a sailor on a dhow from Zanzibar. He called and asked us the time. We replied: Ten-ten. He then became angry and said: What do you mean ten-ten? I ask you the hour of the day. Can't you say twenty? Why this silly ten-ten? And Hamud said: It is known that Negro slaves are among the most ignorant people in the world. In the Muntafiq it is related as follows:

ONCE there were three slaves, and in the night their thoughts were turned to stealing, and they planned to steal sheep from the bedouin who were camped outside the town. In the first hour of the night they went to the camp of the bedouin and they went up to the animals. In the darkness they saw three animals, and each slave took one animal and led it away but they were goats and not sheep, and the slaves knew it not. And the slaves took the goats and went away. But when the goats of the bedouin, which numbered many hundreds, became aware that three goats had gone from them they started to follow them, for it is a custom of the goats that where one goat goes, there must go all the goats.

And the three slaves and the three goats went through the desert, and behind them they heard the sound of many feet. Then the slave Ali said to the slave Rashid: We are pursued. And the three slaves and the three goats ran, and the goats of the bedouin saw the three goats were running, so they, too, ran after them.

And the slave Rashid said to the slave Ali: Truly the bedouin are pursuing us. Then the slaves released the three goats and ran faster, but the goats, after the manner of goats, followed the men. So when the slaves slowed down the goats butted the slave Ali, who was last. And the slave Ali said to the slave Rashid: There are many sharp things prodding me in the posterior. What can they be? And the slave Rashid replied: They are the lances and swords of the Arabs. Run! Run! Though in fact they were not the lances and swords of the Arabs, but only the horns of the goats. But the slaves understood nothing of this affair, so they ran faster and faster until they came to the river. Now, when the goats smelt the river they turned about, for goats have sense, but the leading slave, whose name was Hassan, fell into the river.

And it so happened that in that river was a crocodile, and when the slave Hassan fell in he bit off and ate the head of Hassan the slave. And the slave Ali and the slave Rashid came to the river and they saw that Hassan was in the river and they pulled him out and set him on the bank, but he had no head.

And the slave Ali noticed that Hassan had no head, so he turned and said to Rashid: See, our comrade is without a head. And the slaves are ignorant in these matters, so Rashid replied: Had he then a head before, or has he always been headless? And Ali answered: Truly, I never noticed and I do not remember. And Ali and Rashid discussed the matter between themselves and said: Verily, we must discover the truth of this matter, for if our comrade had a head and has lost it, then he is dead and we must bury him, for it is said amongst the learned that the separation of the head causes the departure of the soul from the body. But if he has always been headless, then he is now no better nor no worse than formerly, and by burying him we may do wrong. So the slave Ali said: Let us ask his mother, for she must have information about the matter.

The slave Ali and the slave Rashid went to the town and they went to the hut of the mother of Hassan and they called: Ya Umm Hassan! And Umm Hassan came and said: What do you want and why trouble me? And Ali asked: O Mother of Hassan, on the day your son was born can you remember, had he a head? And Umm Hassan thought and answered: On that day I was sick and in pain, and it is over twenty years ago and I cannot remember. Then the slave Rashid and the slave Ali went to the father of Hassan and said to him: Ya Aba Hassan! Ya Aba Hassan! When your son Hassan was born, had he a head or was he then headless? And he replied: I have no information concerning this matter, for when my son was born, on that very day, I had gone to Basra to buy coffee, nor did I return till nightfall.

Then the two slaves went to an old woman called Tawa, for Tawa was the midwife. She was a Negro and a slave, but she was the one amongst them who had sense, and she was ignorant of nothing. It is said of her that she could remember even the building of the mosque of Kadhimain. And the slaves Ali and Rashid went to Tawa the midwife and asked of her: O Tawa! When you brought Hassan forth from his mother, had he then a head? And Tawa replied: He had a head, and there was hair on it, and there were eyes in it, and there were ears on it. And they said: O Tawa, now he has no head.What shall we do? And Tawa replied: He is dead. And when Ali and Rashid heard this they wept and beat their chests, and said: Verily our comrade is dead. And Abu Hassan and Umm Hassan heard, and they came, and wept, and beat their chests.

A STORY CONCERNING THE

FOLLY OF JEALOUSY

This story was related at a halt in the desert to prepare tea, near an encampment of the Dhufair, and one of them killed five bustard, and we had none, and it was said, envy and jealousy are attributes of women.

ONCE in Iraq there were two small boys, one of them was the Amir Abdulla, son of the Sultan, and the other was Mohammed, son of the Wazir. And their fathers sent them to school and they stayed in the school for ten years. But in this school the Amir Abdulla learnt nothing. It was his custom only to hit and bully the younger boys, and to play at archery and horsemanship, and the drinking of wine and the pursuit of beauty. And in all these things his companion was Mohammed, son of the Wazir. When they were finished with the school and came out from it the Amir Abdulla had learnt not one single thing. But his friend, Mohammed, had learnt every language which was then spoken in the world, for he was both clever and industrious.

Now, when the son of the Sultan and the son of the Wazir left the school, they could find no work or occupation, for the government of the country was done by their fathers. So it became their custom to ride out at dawn to the high desert, and in the evening to return to the town. And with them as escort rode six Circassian slaves, youths of great beauty, armed with spears and swords. But when they had ridden many miles into the desert the Amir would dismiss the escort, saying: Go back to the town, but return to us here before the setting of the sun.

Then he and the son of the Wazir would spend the day in the pleasures of friendship and companionship. And what the Wazir's son said to the Amir, that suggestion would be adopted by the Amir and done by him, for they were of one heart. The Circassian slaves were jealous of this. They said amongst themselves: What the son of the Wazir tells our master, that he does, but as for us we are neglected. They give us no orders, telling us only to go

23

in the morning and come in the evening, and this state of affairs is not good. What is this constant desert, desert? Therefore we should kill the son of the Wazir that we may put an end to this state. But the Commander of the Circassians said: Why should we do this? It would be a shame to kill him. Rather let us do another thing. Let us go to the witch in the town and explain the affair to her, and let her do magic, that hate may come between these two boys.

So the Circassians went to the witch and said to her: O mistress of wonders, our state is thus and thus; please do magic that these two boys may hate each other. And the witch replied: In this there is no obstacle or difficulty, nor is it necessary to use the knowledge of forbidden books. Give me each of you one dirhem. And the witch took the six dirhems from the Circassians and went to the market. And she bought new clothes and paints and powder for her face and returned to her house. Now this witch was an old hag of more than seventy summers, but such is the artifice of women that when she had applied kohl and put on new clothes, and washed her face with curdled milk, and applied to it paints and powders, she appeared as a young girl of seventeen. But only to one who saw her from many paces away.

And in the morning the witch stood near a mound which lay one hundred paces from the road to the desert. So the two boys rode out of the palace with their Circassian slaves and they saw a young girl, beautiful as a moon, standing on the mound. The young Amir said: I shall have this girl. The son of the Wazir said: No, I shall have her. And the son of the Wazir jumped from his horse and ran towards the mound, and the young girl when she saw him come leapt behind the mound and was hidden from view. Before the Wazir's son arrived on the mound the witch wiped the paint from her face, threw on a dirty cloak, and bared her toothless gums. And she was hideous to behold. The son of the Wazir ran behind the mound and sought the girl, but he could see only the witch. And all around was desert and there was not enough cover for a flea to hide in. And the son of the Wazir was astonished, so slowly he returned to the prince.

Now, the Amir Abdulla called out to Mohammed, son of the Wazir, and asked: Han, Han, and how did it go? Did you kiss her? And the son of Wazir replied: There never was a girl; it was a dream. And the Amir Abdulla, son of the Sultan, did not believe the words of Mohammed, son of the Wazir, and there was anger in his heart. He thought: Is he my friend that he lies to me? Does he imagine me a fool that I should believe this occurrence? And he said to the son of the Wazir: You saw her and you took her in your arms, and these lies are without benefit.

The Amir Abdulla, son of the Sultan, returned to the palace and did not ride out to the desert. And when he was alone he sent for the Commander of his Circassian slaves. And he commanded the officer to go straight to the room of the son of the Wazir and slay him. The Commander of the Circassians said: There is no delay nor hesitation in the execution of the order of a mighty prince, but, O my Lord, he was your friend. May we not imprison him? And the Amir said: Go, or you are slain in his place.

The Commander of the Circassians went out from the palace and killed a cat, for he could not bear to kill the boy. Then he put the blood of the cat on his sword and returned. And the Wazir's son he hid in a secret place. And he went to the Amir and saluted him, saying: This is the sword which executed your most just order. And when the Amir saw the blood he turned pale.

Then the Amir became sad, for he had no friend nor intimate. And he passed the days in melancholy and boredom. And one day he took his slaves and rode out far into the country, until he came to the Persian Gulf, and here he halted on a mound.

And in the distance he saw a ship and it was approaching faster than the wind. There was no horse in Arabia which could equal the speed of that ship. As it approached he saw a girl in it, and she was more beautiful than the flowers of Mosul and purer than the snows of the land of the Kurds. Her body was slim and supple, and as for her breasts, they were the zenith of desire. And the Amir loved her with the strongest love. And the girl saw that the Amir was beautiful like a moon and she signalled to him, for the boat was carrying her with the speed of a bullet. She placed a finger first on her eye, then on her teeth, then on her navel, then on her head. And the Amir did not comprehend her signal. The boat vanished and was gone over the horizon.

And the Amir turned to the Commander of the Circassians and asked: What was the meaning of her signal? And the Commander said: Master, it is hidden from my understanding. And the Amir cried: Fetch me Mohammed, son of the Wazir, for he is the only one in the world who understands every code and every language. And the Commander said: Master, may you never be in that state in which Mohammed, son of the Wazir, now is. And the Amir sighed a great sigh and was overcome with grief, and he said: I have lost my friend and now I have lost her who was destined to be my bride. But a slave crept away and informed Mohammed, son of the Wazir.

And Mohammed came and asked permission to enter into the presence of the Amir, and that thing was allowed and permitted. And the Amir was astonished when he saw the face of his friend, and he ordered that the Commander of the Circassians be rewarded with a thousand dirhems and a beautiful slave girl.

And Mohammed, son of the Wazir, interpreted to the Amir Abdulla, son of the Sultan, the message of the girl. The name of the girl was Ain (the eye), her father was a king, for his strength (the teeth) was second only to the girl's beauty, the name of his kingdom was Surri (the navel), and over his palace was a pomegranate tree.

And the Amir Abdulla sent for ships and for sailors and for soldiers and for treasure, and he left for the kingdom of Surri. And the King of Surri was impressed when he saw his wealth and the beauty of his face. And he took the daughter of the King of Surri in marriage and returned to his country, where he loved her with an exceeding love, and had many sons, beautiful as moons, strong as lions, firm as spears, and brave as is the custom of the Arabs.

And Mohammed the Wazir's son he rewarded with great wealth, and when the Wazir, his father, died he succeeded him and was Wazir in his place.

THE STORY OF THE PRINCE

OF KERMANSHAH AND OF
HIS MISFORTUNES

*And those who tell this story may say that this story was
related by Hussein the Saddler, and he heard it from his mother,
and she was a Persian.*

LET it be known to you that once there was a prince in Kermanshah and he had such wealth as had never been known before in these lands. His escort was a thousand horsemen, and their horses were shod with gold, their horses were of the finest Arab stock, their clothing was of Chinese silk, the leather of their saddles was of the skin of lions, and gold and silver were the only metals used at that Court, save in the blades of their swords, which were of Damascus steel.

And in the course of years that prince took as wife the daughter of the Sultan of the Persians, and she was beautiful as a pearl from Kuweit, nor was there any flaw in her face or in her body, and it was necessary to keep her hidden from the eyes of men, lest after seeing her they became blinded to lesser things, for he who looks into the sun cannot see the glow of a cigarette.

So he took the girl to his palace, and they lived together in pleasure and in joy, and many months passed in the making of love and its enjoyment. And it became apparent that she was with child, and finally a son was born to the prince, and he rejoiced and ordered that there should be such a feast as had never been known before amongst the Persians. And he ordered to be slain a thousand sheep and a thousand geese and a thousand ducks and a thousand peacocks, and they were prepared with rice and limes and walnuts and truffles, and there was laid out a feast so tremendous that it took a man over an hour to ride from one end to the other on a fast horse. And they brought barrels and filled them with the wines of Mosul and the wines of Shiraz and the wines of the Russians and the Franks. And there came kings and princes and nobles and great sheikhs and the heads of tribes and captains of armies and great merchants and they gathered together to

29

honour Rustam, the great prince of Kermanshah, and they ate of the feast and the Prince Rustam also ate of the feast and drank of the wines until he was satisfied.

Now amongst the guests was the Sultan of the Persians, the father of the girl, the wife of Rustam. So when all had laid aside their hands from eating, Rustam rose to give thanks to the Sultan and to the noble guests for their coming. And on the gathering fell a great silence when the prince rose up, that all might hear him with respect. So great was this silence that in the distance could be heard the buzzing of a bee and should a fly alight on the silken tablecloth, then the sound of its alighting was audible to all. Now, as the prince arose he noised a Noise. (May it be far from you.) Now let it not be hidden from you that the Persians have also some civilisation, and amongst them, as amongst us, though a man may sneeze, or cough, and even a belch need not bury him in shame, there is a Noise which none may make without lasting disgrace, and it was this Noise which came from His Highness, the Prince Rustam, Ruler of Kermanshah.

And the Sultan and the great sheikhs and great nobles and merchants and captains heard and were astonished. And from the distance came the sound of a laugh of a slave, for truly slaves are without dignity and they do not know that conduct which is proper and seemly. And the face of the Prince Rustam became black with shame, and he turned from the assembly and went.

And the Prince Rustam returned from that multitude to his palace, nor did he look on the faces of his friends. He took from his treasury a bag of gold and ordered to be saddled his swiftest horse and he prepared for departure. Of all his servants and attendants there came to him only one, and this was a boy, a page, who loved him. And the page Qais said to Rustam, the prince: Permit me to accompany you, O my master. And that thing was permitted him.

So they set forth, intending to reach the lands of the Russians, where the name of the prince and his history would not be known nor rumoured, and they rode on a path through the high mountains, and with them was neither guard nor escort. So it happened when they were traversing the lands of the Kurds that thieves seized the road and attacked them, and these thieves were of the tribes of the Hamavand. And the Prince Rustam drew his sword and as the thieves came he slew them till the road was piled with corpses, and the boy Qais drew his dagger and protected the back of Rustam his master.

But the tribes of the Kurds are numerous. Is it not said, El kurad, jurad (Kurds are locusts)? And in the morning of the second day the Hamavand came and prevailed over Rustam, and he fell wounded to the ground. They took from him his sword and his horse and his bag of gold, and his clothes and his shoes, but they left him lying on the ground, for they thought him dead. And the boy Qais they took to sell as a slave.

In the morning at the rising of the sun Rustam recovered and found himself lying naked on a road in Kurdistan, and he wandered and found a village and asked of them water and they gave it. But when he asked news of Qais the boy they did not answer nor did they comprehend his words. And from village to village he asked until finally the information was accorded him, and they said: There was such a boy as you describe, and he was bought by a rajah of the Hindus, and we saw him in his retinue on the road to India, and he was chained by both hands in a state of nakedness.

Rustam was overcome by sorrow when he heard this news. He took the road to India, but as he had neither money nor wealth he was five years on the journey, for at each town it was necessary for him to halt and work as a porter in the bazaars and the markets to acquire food for the next stage of his journey. And in time he came to Kandahar in the land of the Afghans, and he went to the bazaar and cried to the merchants asking them who was in need of a strong porter.

And one of the merchants, a Jew, hired him and took him to his house, and said: Take these boxes and take them to the hill and put them in the cave. And Rustam took chest after chest and carried them to the hill and put them in a secret cave as directed by the merchant. And the boxes were small but very heavy, so it was clear to Rustam that they contained gold. And when he had carried the last chest to the hill the merchant brought him food and wine to the cave and said: Eat and drink for you are tired.

Now, the merchant thought Rustam to be a peasant from the hills and ignorant of affairs. He did not know him to be of the cleverest of princes. But Rustam thought: Where there is gold, men become as foxes; they do not reveal their lair or their treasure. So he said: O master, it is not seemly that I eat in front of you. So he took the food round a corner in the cave and he made the sound of eating, but he did not eat, and he made the sound of drinking, but he did not drink. And he took up the posture of sleep, but he did not sleep. And he saw the merchant come and there was a dagger in his hand.

And Rustam leapt on the merchant and seized him and the man was as a child in the hands of Rustam the prince. And Rustam slew the merchant. Then he opened the

D

boxes and found them filled with such treasure as surpassed belief. And in them was gold and silver and pearls, and coins of all the kingdoms of the world. And by the time Rustam had counted the treasure night had fallen.

Now, the sons of the merchant became anxious when their father did not return from the hill. One of them said to the other: Evil has befallen our father. And the other replied: It is as you say. Should you see the porter, commit him to the guard, that our father may be avenged and that we may learn the truth.

And in the morning Rustam returned from the cave to the town, and as he passed through the gate the sons of the Jew cried out: Seize this man, for he has killed our father and robbed him. And the guards of the gate seized Rustam and searched his clothing. And his pockets were filled with gold and pearls and precious stones from the treasure of the merchant, and on his shirt was the stain of the merchant's blood. So the guards were convinced and they took Rustam and chained him and led him into the chamber of the Captain of the City Guard.

And the Jews went in and they cried out: O Captain, give us justice, for the porter is truly the slayer of our father. And Rustam was confounded and he thought: How can I escape from this affair? But the Captain of the Guard got up from his chair and he ran to Rustam and embraced him and he kissed him first on one cheek and then on the other cheek and he ordered: Let him be released. So they released Rustam from his chains. And the Captain of the Guard was the boy Qais, page of Rustam the prince, but now a youth of twenty years.

So Qais related his story to Rustam and he said: I was sold in the market to the Hindu Rajah, and along with other slaves I was chained between two elephants and I was in a naked and desperate state, and the Rajah set out on the road to India. And each day we marched for twenty hours, nor could we rest or halt, or they would flog us without mercy or compassion. And there came a night that we halted outside the gate of this city, for the gate was closed until dawn. And they gave to the slaves some grains of corn and some water. And as I was eating of the corn and drinking of the water I saw a rat come up to eat of the corn. And I caught the rat and I held it in my hand. And at the time of the calling of the prayer the sentinels opened the gate and we made ready to pass through, first the Rajah and his soldiers, then the elephant and the chain of slaves connected to the last elephant. And I was the last slave to pass that gate and behind me was the last elephant. But before the last elephant had passed through the gate I slipped the rat down the trunk of that elephant. And the rat ran up inside the trunk into the head of the elephant.

There is no exaggeration nor do I depart from the facts when I say that that elephant became as a mad thing, and it turned and fled, and its strength was the strength of a hundred elephants. Now, the elephant was tied by a chain around its belly, and the other end was secured to the belly of the front elephant, and the front elephant had passed through the gate into Kandahar, and ourselves the slaves were attached to the chain between the two elephants. When the rear elephant turned and rushed madly away the chain grew taut and grew tight, and such was the force of the rush of the rear elephant that the front elephant was lifted off its feet and pulled backwards. But it lodged in the gate of Kandahar as a cork lodges in a bottle, and its feet were clear of the ground; hence there was neither strength nor power in that elephant. And we

35

the slaves were hanging in mid-air from the chain, and such was the tension in that chain that, had it snapped, then surely would we have flown to the lands of the Moroccans. But the chain was of steel and it did not snap. But cracks appeared in the walls of the towers of the gates of Kandahar, though they did not yield. And the guard raised the alarm and the trumpets blew and the troops and the people assembled and cried: There is trickery, the Hindu means to destroy the gate, that an army may come and take the city. And the soldiers of the Afghans fell on the soldiers of the Hindu Rajah and overpowered them, and a great crowd came and assembled in that place.

I was hanging from a chain in mid-air in a naked condition and I called out to the multitude assembled and I cried: We are Moslem youths, believers, enslaved by the infidel and carried in captivity through your land, and is this thing permitted by you or allowed by your laws, O Afghan people? And they replied: The enslavement of believers is neither permitted nor allowed.

Then a high officer rode up to me on a horse and said: O boy, if you are a Moslem, then say the creed. And the Hindu soldiers could neither prevent me nor interfere with me, for they were prisoners. So I said the creed, and the high officer examined me and said: This boy is of the believers. And they brought soldiers and came and killed the elephants, and they brought blacksmiths and freed our chains. And they laid me on the ground, for I was weak to exhaustion from the oppression of the Hindus. Then they carried me to a house and laid me on a bed and rubbed oil on my body, and applied ointments to my back, which was raw from the floggings, and to my wrists, which were eaten to the bone by the iron fetters.

And in the morning we went before the Qadhi and

he heard our story. And he ordered that the treasure of the Rajah should be given to us in compensation, and that the Rajah and his servants and soldiers who were infidels should be sold as slaves. So it came about that I resided in this city and as you taught me much of warlike knowledge I joined the Afghan troops when they went out to fight the Russians and the Hindus, and I was more skilled than any of them. And the King of the Afghans became pleased with me and raised me to this high office.

And Rustam the porter was greatly pleased when he heard the story of Qais the Captain of the Guard, and he related to Qais those facts and those events which are known to you, my listeners, nor did he omit any word of it. And Qais ordered that the sons of the Jew be imprisoned for giving false testimony, and that thing was done to them. Then Qais sent soldiers and brought the treasure of the merchant to the town, and half was given to the poor and to the religious charities and half they kept for their expenses. And to Rustam was given a house and menservants and maidservants and the post of Lieutenant of the City Guard.

And it came about that the King of the Afghans went out to fight the infidel, and Rustam and Qais accompanied his troops. And the Hindus came and they were mounted on elephants and accompanied by tigers and they attacked the army of the faithful. And of the Afghans thousands were slain, and it appeared that defeat was inevitable, for the elephants trampled the Afghans underfoot and the tigers frightened their horses and tore them with their claws.

But such was the wisdom of Rustam in the art of war that he had caused to be caught before leaving Kandahar a thousand hives of bees and these were sealed in earthen

37

pots and carried on the backs of camels. And these pots Rustam now ordered to be placed upon the ground, and he formed a line of pots and behind them he withdrew his troops, and they retired at great speed, and when the Hindus saw them run they followed. And it came about that the elephants knocked over and broke the pots and the bees came out full of anger and vigour. And the bees stung the elephants even beneath their tails, and they stung the tigers and the Hindus. And the elephants and the tigers became mad and fought one with the other, and the Hindus were blinded by the bees and they fled in every direction. And the army of the faithful gathered together and when the bees had all stung their stings, they chased the Hindus and where they found them there they slew them.

And the King of the Afghans was pleased with the stratagem of Rustam, and he ordered him to be rewarded with a robe of honour, and a chest of gold and the command of an army.

And Rustam returned to Kandahar and became one of its most respected and pious citizens, and he took as wife a maiden beautiful as a moon, and had many sons, brave as their father and as skilled as he in the arts of war. And in this manner and in pleasant pursuits forty summers and forty winters passed and Rustam tarried at Kandahar.

There came a day that he rose from his bed and he called for his page and ordered him to bring a looking-glass. And he looked in the glass and saw that his beard was white and his hair was as white as salt. So he sent for his sons and they assembled together, and he said: On every man who makes submission in the Faith of Islam there are laid many tasks and many duties, but when he has travelled for seventy years on the journey of life he is nearing the time for the final unsaddling. And it is this day clear to me that the Angel of Death (may he be far from you) is awaiting me, nor is he patient in his waiting. And the division of my wealth is known to you, my sons, for it is in accordance with the Law. And I have now only one desire left to satisfy, and that is that I may return to my native place, and learn of its state and condition, and die and be buried with fitting ceremonies, for, know you, I am of royal condition, though, for reasons of state, the matter has been a secret.

And Rustam thought: Now after fifty years that unhappy event which caused my departure from Kermanshah will have been forgotten by the people, and I can approach my native place without fear. So he purchased the clothes and the animals of a rich merchant, and he took the name of Abbas Ali es Shirazi and he set out for Kermanshah, nor did he tell anyone his name or station.

And there came a day that he arrived in that plain beside the city of Kermanshah which had been the scene of that ill-omened feast, but the plain which before had been desert was now rich and fertile with crops and in it stood a village where no village had stood before. And Rustam saw and was pleased, and he thought, how well my wife and my son have ruled this country. And he called to a horseman who was coming on the road to ask the name of the village, for he thought: Surely the people will have remembered me. Perchance they have named this village in honour of one of my great victories. And he called out: O Brother, what is the name of this village? And the man answered: This name is known to everyone. The people who live in the village call it Amirabad, that is, Princetown, for so it was named and written in the official records. But we of Kermanshah call it Noiseabad, nor do we refer to it as anything else, for, let it be known to you, the great prince, Rustam the Magnificent, noised the Noise at this place and no other. And Rustam heard the words of the man and was angry and he thought: Will these wretches never forget that event?

But as Rustam went along the road he thought: The people of the bazaars and markets are vulgar people and their thoughts are only of disgusting and common things. But my wife and my son are of royal blood, and such as they think only of pure and dignified things and that disgraceful event will be far from their minds, nor will they be able to recall it. So he went in to the town of Kermanshah, and there he entered a secret passage which was known only to him and to no other in the world, and this passage took him to the council chamber inside the palace. And he stood behind a tapestry in the council chamber, and he could see those who were in that room, yet they were not aware of his presence.

And in that room were seated an old woman, whom Rustam recognised as his beloved queen, and a full-grown man, the image of Rustam in his prime. And before them stood a chamberlain, awaiting their orders. And Rustam was pleased when he saw the faces of those he loved. And the son spoke and said: O Mother, touching on the castles defending our frontier to the north, do they now need garrisons? How long is it since we were attacked by the Russians? And Rustam thought: Now they will recall my name with honour, for it was those Russians that I scattered to the winds. And the woman said: It must be nearly sixty years since they came. And the son answered: Was it before or after the year of the Noise? And the woman answered: The coming of the Russians was five years before the Prince Rustam, your father, noised the Noise. And Rustam heard and was sad, and he thought: There are some matters which shall never be forgotten nor forgiven.

And Rustam turned and left the palace, and he did not speak to his family, and he walked to the top of the high mountain which is near to Kermanshah, seeking the company of animals and birds and those things which do not have memories. And winter came and snow fell on the mountain and Rustam the Magnificent, the noble prince, died of cold on that mountain. But in the spring the shepherds came to the mountain and they found his bones and buried them in a manner suitable to religion. And now in Kermanshah when the children ask: In what year was it that a traveller died in the snow on the high mountain, and was buried by the shepherds, their father will answer: It was fifty years to a year after the mighty prince, Rustam the Magnificent, noised the Noise.

THE STORY OF THE YOUTH

JAMIL, THE SON OF A MERCHANT IN BAGHDAD

Let those who hear this story take heed to their money, when they are in great cities, that it stays with them.

IT is said that in the days of Haroun er Rashid there was a youth named Jamil, and he was the son of a cloth merchant in the bazaar of Baghdad the City of Peace, and only upon God is there belief.

Now, there came a year in which the father of Jamil died, and he was one of the richest merchants in the City of Peace. And Jamil inherited from his father his shop, and the cloths and silks in the shop, and a chest containing gold of such weight that it took twenty men to lift it.

Jamil mourned for his father for many months, and he took his body and buried it in Holy Nejaf, and he returned to Baghdad and sat in the shop to conduct business in place of his father. And in the evenings he used to take a boat, and visit the islands and eat of roast fish and drink arak. But one evening he was passing in his boat when he looked at the window of a house which stood in a garden close to the river and he saw in the window a girl. And he looked at the girl and was amazed, for her skin was of the texture of the petals of lilies, though tinged with the colour of roses. And her eyes were like the gazelle. And her breasts were rounded firmly in that shape which is truly the zenith of perfection, and her waist was as slim as a boy's waist. And Jamil thought: I have no desire and no ambition in life other than that I may love this girl.

So Jamil returned to his house, and he did not go to the islands. And he found a discreet woman who was not accustomed to gossip at the well, and from whom death or torture would not drag a secret. And he said to the sage woman: Go to the street of So-and-So, then go to the house which stands in the garden of pomegranate trees, then speak with the woman servants, and find out from them everything concerning the moon-faced girl who lives in that house, and bring me all information

43

concerning her situation. And in the morning the woman returned from that place and she said: The name of the moon-faced girl is Amira, and she is the daughter of a poor man, a barber, a Persian from Shiraz, and he brought her here as a child—ah, these long journeys are terrible for children. I remember when my father brought me here when I was a child in the hot season, and we travelled on donkeys from Mosul. . . .

But Jamil did not listen to the words of the wise woman, for his mind was on other things and his words cut into her words and he said: Is Amira then married? And the wise woman replied: She is a virgin. And Jamil asked: Has she a cousin or is there anyone with the right to marry her? And the woman answered: There are obstacles to the marriage of this girl. Let it not be hidden from you that she came here a poor girl, then her father died, but she inherited no money from him, yet now she is exceedingly rich and her riches exceed your riches. And Jamil was amazed and he said: You said she was a virgin. From where, then, are these riches?

And the wise woman answered: I said she is a virgin, and it is by discreet and careful enquiries that I am sure of this, for her maidservants and slaves swear even by their eyes that no man has ever even touched her hand. Yet her riches are from her beauty, for her beauty exceeds the beauty of any girl in the City of Peace, and, know you, the rich and those of noble blood will pay even bags of gold to see her, for those of great and royal families love artistic and beautiful things. And this girl will show you her face for fifty dirhems, and her body from the waist upwards clothed in the most beautiful silks for one hundred dirhems, and her whole body clothed in the rarest embroidery of Isfahan for two hundred dirhems, and her body from the waist upwards unclothed for five hundred dirhems, and her whole body unclothed in all its perfection and in every detail for one thousand dirhems, payable in advance. But between you and that girl will be a grid of iron bars as thick as a man's arm, nor can you approach her, and from this position and from this situation and in no other way can you see this girl. And Jamil the Merchant heard and was astonished.

And throughout the night sleep did not come to Jamil the Merchant. He lay on his bed and he thought and considered: How can a way be opened that I may take this girl and marry her, and yet it be unknown to the merchants and to my companions that I have married a girl who has exposed her face to the lustful gaze of desire? But in his thoughts and his dreams no way appeared open before him. And in the morning his desire to see his beloved was strong in him and it overcame him, so he rose from his bed and he went to the bazaar and he went to the shop of one who was skilled in disguises, for he thought: If I am to marry this girl she will be ashamed before me if I know of her profession. And he put on the clothes of a Turkish secretary, and he fastened to his face a beard made of sheep's wool and when he went out from that place his friends knew him not.

And he went to the house which stood in the garden of pomegranate trees and he knocked on the door of the courtyard. And the door was opened by a eunuch of enormous size, armed with a sword. And behind him stood ten more eunuchs, men of great size, armed with swords. And an old woman came out and stood before him. And Jamil the Merchant said to the woman: I wish to see your mistress, the Lady Amira. And the woman replied: In what manner do you wish to see my mistress?

45

Do you wish to see her face, or her body from the waist upwards clothed in the richest silks, or her whole body clothed in the rarest cloth of Isfahan, or in what manner and in what condition do you wish to see my mistress?

And Jamil the Merchant replied: I do not want to gaze on your mistress in this manner, I wish only to converse with her on affairs of importance beyond your comprehension. And the woman answered: It is neither permitted nor allowed. And she made a sign to the eunuchs, who advanced upon Jamil the Merchant. And Jamil the Merchant said: Take, then, fifty dirhems; I will see the lady's face. So the woman took the money and she unlocked a door in the wall and she took Jamil the Merchant up a narrow staircase, guarded by eunuchs armed with swords, and she left him in a small chamber which had in one wall an opening guarded by a grid of bars of iron as thick as a man's arm. And through this opening he could see a room furnished in the richest manner. And the woman warned him as she left: Have no speech with my mistress, or a shutter will fall and she will vanish from your sight.

And Jamil the Merchant waited in that chamber, and his heart was beating fast and loud. Then a door opened and behind the iron bars appeared the face of the Lady Amira, his beloved. And Jamil the Merchant saw and was astonished. For he saw that her ears were like the petals of a flower, and her forehead was the colour of milk, and her cheeks were like ripe peaches, her lips were the acme of desire, and as for her eyes, when he looked into them he lost the power of thought. And in this manner Jamil the Merchant gazed on the face of his beloved. There was no power of reason in him and he spoke and said: O my lady, I am sent to you by my master, a wealthy merchant of Stambul, and he desires to marry you, and he will give

46

you a chest of gold, and rich cloth, and anything in the world that you desire if you will leave Baghdad and go to that place and wed him. But the Lady Amira made a sign and an iron shutter fell behind the iron bars and he was cut off from her sight. And Jamil the Merchant left that chamber and he left that room and his heart was heavy with grief. And he returned to his shop, but he did no trade, for all sense had left his brain.

And the next day and the following day and on every day he went to the house which stood in the garden of pomegranate trees and on every day he gave the woman a thousand dirhems that he could gaze on his beloved naked in all her beauty. And each time he tried to speak to his beloved the shutter would fall and he would be cut off from her sight. And in this manner six months passed, and Jamil the Merchant was ruined, and his shop was empty of cloths and rich stuffs.

And when his money was finished Jamil the Merchant dressed in the guise of the Turkish secretary and he went to the house that stood in the garden of pomegranate trees and he said to the woman: It is many hundreds of times that I have visited this house, and the money given me by my master the Ottoman Pasha is finished, yet I have not executed his orders. Let me out of mercy and compassion see your mistress, that I may conclude my business. But the woman made a sign to the eunuchs, and they advanced on Jamil the Merchant and they seized him and they threw him out of the courtyard into the dust of the road and they beat him with whips and with sticks and he lay in the road in a bleeding and miserable state. And the woman servant came to him and spoke in this manner: Go from here, O dog of the Ottomans, and remain far from us, for my mistress is revenged on you as she will be

47

revenged on the whole tribe of Adam. For, know you, my mistress is of royal blood and her father was a king in Fars, but through the treachery of his ministers and his soldiers his kingdom was overthrown and he had to fly from the land. But the Queen, the mother of my mistress, a lady of unsurpassed beauty, was caught by the treacherous Wazir, and he did to her things which it is not permitted to mention, and finally he killed her in an atrocious manner, and when my mistress reached the age of reason and became aware of these facts she resolved to employ her beauty, her only weapon, to ruin men, for in men she saw only evil and treachery, while goodness and virtue are reserved for women. And Jamil the Merchant heard the words of the woman servant and he rose from the ground and he returned to his shop and his heart was heavy with grief. And he sat in his shop weeping, and his shop was empty of cloths and rich stuffs.

Now, it happened that on that very day Abu Nawas, friend and companion of the Commander of the Faithful, was passing through the market in disguise, thinking to find some play or jest which might amuse his master and divert his thoughts from the cares of state and which might make him happy. And as he was passing the shops of the great merchants laden with the silks and rich stuffs and embroideries of Damascus and of China he saw a shop which was empty of cloth or goods, and in it was seated a youth of great beauty who was weeping in a manner which tore the heart.

And Abu Nawas went up to the youth and he saluted him and said: He! He! O boy, what is it that you sell? Is it your beauty, for I see you have no other goods with you? And Jamil the Merchant answered him and said: Depart from me, O my master, as from one afflicted by the plague, for there is no power or reason in me, and I see nothing before my eyes but the face of a girl, nor can I engage in any trade or occupation. It is only the Angel of Death who can bring release from this torture. But Abu Nawas seated himself in that shop and he plied the youth with questions until he had related all those facts and those events which are known to you, my listeners, nor was a single word omitted from the account. And Abu Nawas heard the story of Jamil and he thought: This will develop into a fine story for the amusement of my master.

And Abu Nawas said to Jamil the Merchant: O boy, your history wrings sympathy from the heart, but you have conducted this affair and dealt with this matter in a manner natural to youth. Wisdom and experience will gain for you all that your heart desires. Therefore, if you will follow me in everything you will regain fortune. Only you must follow me and do everything that I do and imitate my actions so long as my right eye be open, but when I close my right eye, then you must do nothing and abstain from every action and every deed until your desires are fully gained.

Abu Nawas took Jamil the Merchant to the shop of disguises, and they both put on clothes similar to those of the Chinese, but Abu Nawas left the face of the boy Jamil bare of disguise in all its beauty. Then they went to the river and Abu Nawas produced a bag of gold and bought a boat. Then Abu Nawas purchased a donkey of the most powerful breed and he harnessed it to the boat with ropes, but he did not put the boat in the river. Then Abu Nawas and Jamil the Merchant seated themselves in the boat and the donkey dragged the boat over the sands and mud by the side of the river and they went in the direction of the house which stood in the garden of

E

pomegranate trees. And when they came near to that house Abu Nawas began to sing in this manner:

Aba Daba, Aba Daba,
Daba Aba, Daba Aba,
Aba Daba, Aba Daba.

And, imitating him, Jamil the Merchant sang also this strange song. And in this manner Abu Nawas and Jamil the Merchant passed by the house which stood in the garden of pomegranate trees. And a window opened and the face of the maidservant appeared at it, and Abu Nawas and Jamil the Merchant heard her call out to her mistress: Come, O mistress, there are strange men travelling over the land in a boat. Come and see this comedy. And the lovely face of the girl Amira appeared at the window, nor was it covered by a veil. And Abu Nawas said to Jamil: Look well at that face, for the fifty dirhems have not left your pocket.

Then Abu Nawas halted the donkey and he got down from the boat, and he took from the boat rice and meat and cooking-pots and he collected wood and he lit a fire. But he lit the fire in the cooking-pot and he put the rice under the cooking-pot, nor was it in any vessel, nor was it immersed in water. And the girl Amira said to the maidservant: See how these men cook. The rice is not in water, nor will it be heated by that fire. How, then, can this rice be eaten? And after the food had been under the fire for ten minutes Abu Nawas said to Jamil the Merchant: Come, brother, the food is cooked, we will eat. Then Abu Nawas took a handful of rice and poured it into the neck of the shirt of Jamil and, imitating him, Jamil took of the rice and poured it into the neck of Abu Nawas.

And the girl Amira saw and was amazed, and she said to the maid: We will go down and amuse ourselves with this affair, for stranger sight was never seen. And the girl Amira and her maidservant came out from the house which stood in the garden of pomegranate trees and they came up to Abu Nawas and Jamil the Merchant and saluted them and said: Welcome, O strangers, and forgive us for our interest in your ways and customs, for we are but two foolish women and we have never seen such strange ways before. What manner of men be you, and from what land?

And Abu Nawas replied to her and answered her in this fashion: Know, O Lady, that we are from a land which lies beyond China, and it is so far over the sea from China that it has never been visited by the Arabs, and our king is the great King Aba Daba, the munificent, the wise, and so great is his wisdom that he has laid down rules for our conduct in conformity with philosophy, and the punishment for breaking them is death. He has ordained that since fire is one of the most powerful elements able to consume even books containing wisdom itself, the placing of food over it is insulting and ungracious. And such is his wisdom that he has ruled that the riding of animals is heathen, since it puts man over an animal made by God, and he has ordained that wheels are evil since they are loved by the fiend Iblis, who abhors straightness, and what could be more curved and less straight than a wheel? Wheels and riding being forbidden us, we travel in boats in this fashion, whether on water or dry land, and if you ask why we eat by stuffing the rice down the necks of our shirts, who could put dry rice into his mouth?

And the girl Amira and the maidservant laughed much at the words of Abu Nawas, and they were astonished at what they heard, and they said: Permit us, O strangers, to bring you food which has been delicately cooked, that

51

you may be refreshed after your travels. And Abu Nawas answered her and said: We are grateful and we accept, but on one condition, that you yourselves take the food and pop it into our mouths. For, know you, our master the king, Aba Daba, has a magic glass into which he looks and sees his subjects wherever they may be, but you he cannot see, for you are not of his land. Were he to see our hands go to our mouths, then he would suspect that we were eating food which has been over a fire, but your hands are invisible to him.

And the girl Amira and her maidservant returned to the house which stood in the garden of pomegranate trees and they commenced to prepare food. They killed a sheep and they killed a goose and they killed a chicken and a pigeon and a lark. They cooked the sheep and they cooked the goose and they put the goose inside the sheep and the chicken inside the goose and the pigeon inside the chicken and the lark inside the pigeon. And they put the meat on a mound of the finest amber rice cooked in the most delicate manner with saffron and with truffles. And the girl Amira said to the maidservant: If there is goodness and virtue in men, then it is in that youth, for his face has the beauty of paradise.

And when the food was prepared Amira and her maidservant carried it out to Abu Nawas and to Jamil. Night had fallen and the world was dark, save for the light of the stars and the new moon. And they carried out to them also the finest and most delicate wine. Then the maidservant fed Abu Nawas by popping the food into his mouth and the girl Amira fed Jamil by popping the food into his mouth, and Abu Nawas and Jamil drank of the wine and were satisfied.

Then Abu Nawas put his arm around the maidservant

and he kissed her. And the girl Amira looked at Jamil and saw his beauty, and her heart was full of love, and she said: Do to me as your friend is doing to my servant. But Jamil looked at Abu Nawas and saw that his right eye was closed, so he did not follow his example and he replied: Know, fair girl, that kissing is not allowed by our great King, Aba Daba, until an examination has been passed in its art, and this examination is held once every five years in the presence of the King and the Court. For Aba Daba holds that kissing is a most important matter and must be done in the proper manner. Now, my friend has passed the examination and holds a certificate permitting him to kiss whom he will, but, as for me, I never had the chance to take this examination. And should Aba Daba, our great King, look into his magic glass and see my lips go through the motions of kissing, even though you are invisible to him, he would suspect your presence, and on my return to our country my punishment would be that I would have to kiss an iron bar, heated to white heat, until my lips are entirely burnt away.

The girl Amira heard the words of the youth Jamil and she was astonished and her heart was sad, and she watched Abu Nawas kissing her maidservant. And Abu Nawas kissed the maidservant with the most passionate kisses and his hand parted her robe and he opened her dress and took it from her, and truly, O my listeners, modesty forbids me from further mention of this affair.

And the girl Amira looked at Abu Nawas and at her maidservant and she said to the youth Jamil: Do to me as your friend is doing to my servant. And Jamil looked at Abu Nawas and he saw that his right eye was closed. So he said: Sweet girl, know you that Aba Daba our great King holds this art even more important than the art of kissing and the examination is a severe one, and though my friend is an accomplished master holding a certificate of distinction, I have never taken the examination nor passed the test. And were Aba Daba to look through his magic glass and see me doing this thing without a certificate of proficiency, then on my return to my country my punishment would be that they would take me and shut me in a cage with a roaring tigress and they would say: Do unto the tigress as you did to that girl. But in this matter no man has yet been successful and all have perished. And the girl Amira heard the words of the youth Jamil and she was astonished and her heart was sad.

But Abu Nawas spoke and said: If you desire this thing there is only one solution and only one road open to you, and that is that the youth should never return to the country of our great king Aba Daba, but his riches and his wealth in that country will be lost to him. However, if you, O maid, will sign a paper giving him your house and your land and your gold and your furniture and rich stuffs and everything that is yours, and if you promise to marry him, then he can do that which you desire without fear of the consequences.

And the girl Amira looked at Jamil, the youth, and her love for him was great. So Jamil produced paper and pens and the document was written and was signed by the girl Amira and witnessed by Abu Nawas and the maidservant. And the merchant Jamil took the girl Amira and married her in accordance with the law. And Abu Nawas returned to the Palace and related all these events to the Commander of the Faithful, who laughed heartily at these events. And he ordered that Jamil the Merchant should be granted a high office at Basra, and Abu Nawas he rewarded with a bag of gold.

THE STORY OF THE LOST SOUL

I related that ancient story told in Arab Palestine of three men who went to sell arak. One of the men said to another: I have a piastre in my pocket, I will be the first customer. And he gave the piastre to the other man and took a glass of arak. Then this other man said to the third man: I now have a piastre; sell me a glass of arak. And the third man, when he had the piastre, gave it to the first man and asked for a glass of arak, and they went on in this manner until they were drunk and the arak was finished and their profit was only one piastre.

AND Hussein continued:

It is also said that once in Basra were three slaves, and they used to steal vegetables from the gardens and sell them, and when they had the money they would go to the wineshop and mix wine with arak and arak with kanyak, that they might become drunk beyond the bounds of drunkenness.

And one evening they had been doing this very thing and they came out from the wineshop into the street, and there came towards them a high officer of the Ottomans, a Pasha, who was walking through the town in search of pleasures and amusement. And one of the slaves, Jaffer, who was far gone in drunkenness, ran up to the Pasha, and put his arms around his neck and threw him to the ground, saying: O high Pasha, exalted is your estate and you are put over us even by the Sultan himself, and I am only a poor Negro. Yet I am standing over you and you are beneath me and I marvel at this state of affairs. But the Pasha rose to his feet and drew his sword and he struck the slave Jaffer a mighty blow. So he fell to the ground, and the Pasha departed and left them.

And the slave Hamed said to the slave Ali: Our comrade is hurt. Run and get a surgeon, so much blood is flowing from him. And the slave Ali ran and brought a learned surgeon who examined the slave Jaffer who was lying on the ground. And the surgeon turned to them and said: You have brought me here without reason and without cause, for though this wound is not beyond my skill to repair and heal, for I am the most skilful surgeon in Basra and in all Iraq, and there is no wound so great that I cannot repair it, yet there is one small matter with which I am unable to deal and for which I have no skill, and that is that in this body there is no soul, and the soul has indeed

57

come out from it. And with these words the surgeon left them and returned to his house.

And the two slaves Hamed and Ali discussed the words of the surgeon and said: There is only one way to help our comrade and that is to find his soul and put it in the body, that the wise surgeon may heal his wound and he may be as before. For truly the slaves are ignorant of matters concerning religion. And the slave Hamed said to the slave Ali: Where shall we find the soul of our comrade Jaffer? And Ali replied: He had no money, therefore he will have gone to the gardens to steal vegetables that he may sell them and enjoy himself.

So the two slaves went to the gardens, and when they approached them they heard an uproar and a commotion. And the slave Ali asked one of the Arabs, the fellahin: What is the meaning of this noise? And the Arab answered and said: A large black Thing came out of the night and it tore up vegetables and did great great damage, but exactly what it was we could not see in the darkness, except that it was large and black. And the slave Hamed said to the slave Ali: Surely this Thing was the soul of our friend Jaffer, since it was large and black. And the slave Ali replied: Verily it was he, but now where shall we find him? And the slave Hamed said: Since he now has vegetables which he can sell for money, where else shall we find him but at the house of Habiba the Courtesan? And Ali said: Verily you are right.

The slave Ali and the slave Hamed went to the house of Habiba the Courtesan, and they tried the door, and they found it locked. And the slave Ali picked up an iron bar which lay by that door, and he beat upon the door, and both the slaves cried out to Habiba the Courtesan to open the door. Now, let it be known to you that Habiba the

58

Courtesan was not alone in that house, for with her was a high officer, a Bey, holding office of dignity amongst the Ottomans who ruled Basra. And the Bey, the Turk, went to the window and looked out and he saw the two slaves belabouring the door crying out to Habiba to open the door. And from that house there was no escape save through that very door.

And the Bey thought after this fashion: These slaves appear drunk and excited and if I go out through that door I may be involved in a quarrel with them. And though I may kill them or call the guard and have them arrested, the matter will become known throughout the town, and my wife will ask me: What were you doing in the house of Habiba? And my friends will talk and laugh at me in the coffee-house, and when I enter amongst them and salute them the talk will grow silent and all eyes will look at me. Rather will I do a clever thing. I will dress myself in a bed sheet and make myself as a ghost, for these Negroes are fearful, superstitious creatures, and when they see a ghost they run in panic, and I may return to my house with peace and dignity. So the Bey took a bed sheet and wrapped it around himself, and Habiba applied charcoal to his face, and he was terrible to behold. And he opened the door and went out with an awesome shriek.

The slave Ali and the slave Hamed saw the ghost come out from the house of Habiba the Courtesan and the slave Ali cried: It is the soul of our friend. The slave Hamed cried: It is not the soul of our friend, for his soul is black and this one is white. But he shouted too late, for Ali, to stop the ghost, had hit it a mighty blow on the head, and that ghost sank to the ground and became as a dead thing. And Habiba the Courtesan saw this and came out and

59

cursed them, saying: Know what you have done, fools. You have slain the Ottoman Bey, even the Bey of the Gendarmerie himself. Now take this body and remove it far from my house, that I may not become involved in this affair.

And the slaves Ali and Hamed removed the sheet and they saw that the Bey was even as in the grip of death, and Ali said: I am astonished that we were in search of a soul without a body and we have found a body without a soul. And they asked: But where can we take this body? For wherever we leave it in the town, the Turks will find it, and they will say: The Arabs have slain the Bey of the Gendarmerie. Nor will they cease from arrests and torture until they discover the truth of this matter. And Habiba said: Wrap the body in a blanket and tie it up after the manner of a corpse, and take it to the serai. For there is halted near there a caravan from Persia carrying bodies for burial in the holy soil of sacred Nejf. There you may leave this body, for the camels will be unloaded for the night, and you may leave this body with the other bodies, and in the morning they will not notice that there is one body too many, and they will load it up and take it away and bury it in holy Nejf.

And Ali and Hamed put the body of the Turk in a blanket and bound it with ropes after the manner of corpses and took it to the caravan which was halted near the serai. And the camels were unloaded for the night and the corpses had been piled in a big pile, and there was no guard nor sentry over them. For who would steal this merchandise?

And the slaves put the body of the Bey in that pile, but they put him underneath and they piled on him corpses that the fresh corpse might not be on top. And the two slaves, Ali and Hamed, left him and went off to search for the soul of their comrade, Jaffer.

Now, the Turkish Bey had not been killed by the blow of Ali the slave, but only stunned by it, and after a time his senses returned to him, and he found himself bound in a blanket and he could not move either hand or foot. And he breathed and smelled the smell of corpses, nor could he perceive any other odour.

And he thought: Verily, I am slain, and they have put me with the bodies and they are going to bury me. But my life has been a wicked life and shortly I shall be examined on my fitness to enter paradise. And the Bey wept and his heart was full of repentance, and he commenced to recite verses from the Holy Quran.

Now, the owner of the caravan was in his tent, a Persian from Shiraz, and he was calculating the profit which he would have from the bodies, for the relations and heirs of the dead had paid him a sum of money to transport the bodies from Shiraz to Nejf, and to buy a plot of land in which to bury them, and some had paid a lot of money for expensive land near to the holy shrine and others had paid a little money for land far removed from it, and they had also paid for the expenses of burial and had given donations for the holy shrine. And the Persian caravaneer had the record of these sums in his book.

And he thought: If I continue this journey to Nejf and disburse all these various sums, then the profit which will remain for me will be small, and it will not recompense me for all this trouble and the everlasting smell of these corpses. Rather should I do another thing, I should dump these bodies in the high desert where none may see them, and the jackals and the vultures will have a profit from them. And this course is easy for me, save that the camel men are from Shiraz, and on their return they may speak of this event to my destruction at the hands of the loving relatives.

And the Persian thought and thought and a way appeared open to him and he thought thus: At the next halt tomorrow night, let us camp far out in the desert away from towns or villages, and this course will appear reasonable to the camel men, since this caravan is not likely to attract thieves. And the camel men will prepare their food in the large pot, and I will say: Put also this meat in the pot. And I will throw in a piece of meat containing poison, and in the morning there will be twenty more corpses. But what is twenty amongst so many corpses? Then I will lead off the unladen camels, for there will be no need to saddle them, to the nearest Arab village, where I will sell them, and then with my profit I will return to Shiraz. I will say to the people: The dead are buried in accordance with religion, and the camel men died of cholera on the road, and them also I buried in holy Nejf and the fees and charges for their burial are such and such.

And the Persian was musing in this manner when one of the camel men burst into his tent and cried: O Master, the dead are reciting the Holy Quran. And the Persian was seized with fear, and he dashed out of his tent to the pile of corpses, and he heard a voice reciting the Holy Quran come from that pile of corpses. His face turned white and he trembled, thinking: My thoughts were known to the dead.

Now, the Bey was being stifled by the corpses on top of him, and he could not bear their smell, and he thought: These corpses are surely the corpses of the lowest type of men, for how could the corpses of men of dignity and position smell in this manner? But my corpse is the corpse of a Bey, and a large multitude should follow it in the funeral procession. It must be some mistake that I have been put with these men. And the Bey tried to extricate himself from the pile of corpses, but was unable to move either hand or foot. However, he found he could wriggle in the manner of a legless grub, and in this manner he came out of the pile.

When the Persian and the camel man saw the corpse leave the pile they began to scream, and they were filled with horror and could not move from that spot. And the Bey heard their cries and made towards the sound. And the Persian and his camel man saw the corpse come wriggling towards them over the ground and their horror knew no bounds. Power to move returned to them and they started to run, and as for the camel man, he stopped when he had gone a few miles from the town. But the Persian owner of the caravan was still running when he passed Nasiriyat el Ahwaz, a hundred miles away nor was he ever afterwards heard of in Basra, and some say that God deprived him of his reason.

Now, when the Persian and the camel man ran away the Bey was left lying on the ground and wriggling after the manner of a legless grub. And his head hurt from the blow and his arms and legs hurt from the ropes which bound him tightly. And it came into his mind that he could not be a corpse to feel pain in this manner, and he realised that he had been tied in the blanket in the manner of a corpse when he was lying stunned. So the Bey did not know how to extricate himself from this situation, and he wriggled slowly down the street and the time was the sixth hour of night.

Now, those who were passing in that street and who saw the corpse come wriggling down the street were stricken with panic and they fled from very fear. And the Bey went on until he heard music from a doorway, and he knew that the place was the Hall of Pleasure where the great Pashas and the noble Beys congregated in the evenings to watch the dancing of girls and the dancing of boys and to listen to music and to pass the night in pleasures and delights. So he entered that door and wriggled through even into the centre of the Hall of Pleasure. And the music stopped and every eye regarded the corpse which lay in the centre of the hall. And about the Bey was the authentic odour and aroma of death, for he had lain among the corpses. So the great Pashas and the noble Beys held the sleeves of their gowns to their noses, and in their hearts was a great fear.

The Bey knew exactly who would be in the Hall of Pleasure gazing at the girls and the boys, though he could see them not, and he knew their ranks and he knew their names, for he was their friend and he was often of that company.

So he spoke, and his voice was even as a voice from the tomb, and he named by name everyone who was sitting there, and he named them by their ranks and by their station, and their faces were pale with fear. And he said: O mighty Pashas, O noble Beys, O Ottoman comrades, know you that I am Talaat Pasha. I died twelve months ago of a colic at this very Hall of Pleasure, and you were at my funeral. Know you that I am returned from the tomb by express sanction of the Angel of Death, and my desire is to warn you of the evil which awaits you, for you do not say the prescribed prayers. You drink forbidden wines and you engage in evil pleasures. And then

64

F

the Bey named each of them again by name and he related after each name the vices of that man, and the great Pashas and the noble Beys sat trembling in their seats.

And the Bey commanded them: Go instantly from here and go to the Mosque, and there shall you pray until the first light of dawn. Then shall you go to your houses and take a tenth of your wealth and give it to the poor, and never again shall you enter this abode of wine and sin.

And the Pashas and Beys departed from that Hall of Pleasure, nor did they linger or tarry. And the Hall was deserted except for the dancing boys and dancing girls, and he said, naming them by name: In you there is less evil than there is in them, and I desire of you only that you shall carry me to a chamber, and lay me on a bed and cut these ropes, for I must return now to my master. But you shall not lift the blanket which covers me on pain of instant death, for none can gaze on my face and live. But the dancing girls and dancing boys shrank from him, nor did they desire to touch the Bey. But the Bey ordered them in a terrible voice: Lift me or I must summon my master, the Angel of Death, and if he comes who knows who he will take back with him?

So they lifted him and put him on a bed in a private chamber and they cut the ropes. And the Bey commanded them: Go now, and leave this building and do not return before sunrise, for dreadful things will happen here this night. And so they left him. The Bey threw off the blanket and left the room and left the Hall of Pleasure and he returned to his house in dignity and peace, nor was anyone aware of his misfortunes.

After the two slaves, Ali and Hamed, had left the Bey on the pile of corpses they continued their search for the soul of their friend, the slave Jaffer. And they went through

66

the streets of Basra, but they could not see the black soul of their friend.

Now, it so happened that a large black bear had escaped from a juggler that very night, while he was leading it on a chain through the city of Basra, and it was this bear and no other which was the large black Thing which had stolen the vegetables from the garden. But the slaves had no knowledge of this, nor had they ever seen a bear, for slaves are ignorant creatures. And they debated one with the other as to where they could find the soul of their friend. And the slave Ali said: He was not at the house of Habiba the Courtesan. Where can he be? The slave Hamed answered: Since he will have money from the vegetables he has stolen and he was not at the house of Habiba the Courtesan, then the only place he can be is at the wineshop, and we were fools not to go there before.

The two slaves went to the wineshop, and when they approached it they saw that its chairs and benches and tables were overturned and in disorder, and the glasses and bottles and jars of arak and kanyak and wine were smashed and broken on the floor, and there was a large pool of liquor which had come from every jar and every bottle mingled together and from the pool the large black bear was drinking. And the slave Ali said to the slave Hamed: That large black Thing which is drinking the liquor is surely the soul of our friend. But the slave Hamed replied: We must be careful. May it not be the soul of the dead Bey? For he was an Ottoman, his soul will be very black, and the Ottomans also love drinking. The slave Ali answered: See how he drinks by mixing the arak and the kanyak and the wine. That is the way Jaffer used to drink, but the Beys and Pashas sip delicately at kanyak or at wine. That is the soul of our friend and no other.

The two slaves went up to the bear and they caught it by the chain which was about its neck and they led it off, saying: Come, Jaffer, come back into your body. The bear was very drunk, but the slaves pushed it and pulled it until they got it back to the body of the slave Jaffer. The slave Ali then asked: How are we going to put it back into the body, through the mouth or through the nose or through the ears or through the wound, in what way shall we put it back? And all their attempts to put the soul into the body failed, and the bear lay down and went to sleep, for it was very drunk.

And there was wine in Hamed and Ali also, and there was no sense in them. Hamed said: There is only one way in which we can succeed in this affair. Let us shut up the soul and the body in a room and lock the door. When the soul sees no way out of that room perhaps he will enter the body of his own accord, and meanwhile we will go off and fetch the cleverest magician and bring him here. Then if, when we open the door, the soul is still not in the body, he will know what to do. So Ali and Hamed locked the door on the body and the bear and they went off to search for the cleverest magician in Basra.

For a time the bear slept like a dead thing, but at length it awoke with a great hunger and a great thirst, for its appetite had been increased by the kanyak, the arak, and the wine. It searched the room, but could find neither food nor drink, only the body of Jaffer. Now, bears like to eat corpses, so it ate the body of Jaffer, and swallowed it completely, nor did any part of it remain.

When Ali and Hamed had found the house of the cleverest magician in Basra they roused him from his bed and brought him to the room. They unlocked the door and he entered. Then the magician saw the state and condition of the bear and he realised the truth behind the story the slaves had told him and he said: The soul has not entered the body; rather the body has entered the soul.

THE STORY OF MAQDAD—HE

WAS THE HERO OF HILLA

And this story was related between the setting of the sun and the rising of the moon, when there was no light to travel by. The storyteller was Abed.

THERE was or there was not in ancient times a boy living near to Hilla, and only on God is there belief. Now, the name of this boy was Maqdad. He was the son of a great warrior, but his father was slain in battle, and there was no one to bring money or food to their house. So the boy Maqdad hired himself out to the shepherds and he used to take the sheep out in the morning and bring them back at night, and he earned enough to buy a little food for his mother and himself.

One day, when he reached the age of sixteen years, his mother called him, and told him to open a great chest which lay in their house. He opened the chest and found in it a sword of the finest Damascus steel with a hilt of gold, and a shield of leather and iron, studded with gold, a great spear, a dagger wrought in silver, a rich saddle, a mace of the finest teakwood, studded with iron, and all the accoutrements of a warrior.

Then Maqdad's mother said to him: On that wretched day that your father was carried dead into our house I took these weapons from him and from his horse and cleansed them of his blood, and set them in this chest, that one day you might be a mighty warrior in his place. And here is a bag of gold which I took from his body, and I have not spent a single coin from it, though in all these years we have never eaten meat, but only dates and rice and milk and that food which is suitable for the poor. Now take this bag of gold and buy the best horse in the land. Then shall you ride out to the north. For know you that the army of the Shah of the Persians is camped upon the River Tigris, and the Arabs of the great tribes, of Al Fetla, of As Shammar, of Ed Dulaim, are riding against the Persians and are raiding and harrying them that they may be driven from this Arab land

71

So Maqdad took the bag of gold and he went to the market in Hilla where there were offered for sale horses of the finest stock and of the finest blood. And there he saw a horse of between two and three years, and its colour was as black as jet and its beauty surpassed the beauty of all horses, and the horse looked at Maqdad with a look of friendship and affection. So Maqdad turned to the merchant and said: What is his price? Now, the merchant looked at Maqdad and saw that he was dressed as a ragged shepherd boy and he laughed and said: O master of wealth, begone from here and do not trouble us further, for we are afraid that you will offer us so much gold that we cannot lift it from the ground, for we are poor and feeble. Please go from here and do not tantalise us further with your wealth.

Maqdad was angered at the scorn of the merchant and he said: My wealth is greater than your wealth, and I wager you a wager that my purse has more gold than your purse, and the stake shall be my purse against your purse. And the merchant thought: Verily God has deprived this boy of his reason, but let us amuse ourselves and draw a crowd, for it will be good for business. So the merchant called for witnesses, and a crowd collected, and the conditions of the wager were cried out.

Then the merchant drew from his pocket a mighty purse and he said to Maqdad: Let us see your money. And Maqdad's heart went cold when he saw the size of the merchant's purse, and he drew out his own purse and it was smaller than the merchant's. And the merchant spread his coins on a carpet and they saw that there were five hundred dinars of gold and a thousand dirhems of silver and two thousand fils of copper. And Maqdad spread out his coins on the carpet and they saw that he had

72

a thousand dinars in gold, and he had not a single coin in silver or in copper. And the witnesses said: The shepherd boy wins the wager.

Maqdad took the purse of the merchant and put the coins of gold and silver with his own gold, but the copper coins he caused to be thrown to the poor. And he turned to the merchant and asked the price of the horse, and a price was agreed on and paid. Then Maqdad asked the merchant for the pedigree of the horse and for his name. The merchant was astonished, and asked: Do you ask the pedigree of the horse after the price has been agreed and paid? Maqdad replied: His pedigree is written in his legs and his back and his noble head, but it must also be recorded on paper, and that is what I require. And the merchant handed the pedigree to Maqdad, saying: Verily he is descended from the Prophet's noble mare, the feather coated, the most beautiful of all. His name is Rishan, for he is of that noble breed.

Maqdad took the horse Rishan and mounted him bareback and rode to his home. And his mother brought out the saddle of his father and it fitted the horse Rishan, and she brought out the weapons which she had cleaned till they gleamed in the sun. And she brought him a bag of dates and a bag of cheese and she said: Now shall you ride to the Tigris and to the camp of the tribes, and there shall you enter the guest tent and salute the assembly, and they will bid you to be seated and bring for you coffee. Then they will ask your name, for they do not know your face, then shall you reply: I am Maqdad son of Thamir son of Degaither son of Mansur son of Maqdad son of Degaither son of Mansur son of Qais son of Hamed the Lame son of Mansur the Father of the Sword. And this name is a known name, and wherever you say it, there shall you be

73

recognised. For your father was a warrior, and your grandfather, and your great-grandfather and all those before him were warriors. Then Maqdad kissed his mother and bid her farewell. And Umm Maqdad wept as she saw her son depart.

Maqdad rode out and took the road to the north and he rode over the desert which was carpeted with the flowers of spring, and the grace and pace of Rishan was beyond compare. As they went over the desert Maqdad would take his great spear and hurl it in front of him a distance of two hundred paces, and he would put Rishan to a gallop and catch the spear and pluck it from the air before it could touch the ground. In this manner they had travelled many miles when Maqdad saw a gazelle. He put Rishan to a gallop, thinking: Rishan is faster than the gazelle. The gazelle left the track and went off into the desert with Maqdad in pursuit, and Rishan was as fast as the gazelle and drew level with it. But when Maqdad put out his spear to kill it, it turned more sharply than the horse, and in this manner escaped them.

They were now far from the track, and to return to it Maqdad took his course from the wind, and they travelled on and came to a wadi which was both wide and deep, and in its further bank Maqdad saw a cave. The mouth of this cave was covered by a net, its shape as a spider's web, but each strand was as thick as a man's wrist, and through the meshes of the web it could be seen that in the cave was a boy. He was naked save for an iron band around his neck, and he was chained to the wall, and he was in the twelfth year of his life.

Then Maqdad rode down into the wadi; he dismounted and drew his sword, and he cried out to the boy: I will release you from this misfortune. The boy answered, saying: Return from where you have come, O noble stranger, lest my misfortune become your misfortune, for that web is of magic and evil materials. But Maqdad did not heed the words of the boy, and he slashed with his sword at the web. But as he cut each strand the severed ends grew and became longer and came out and seized the legs and arms of Maqdad and drew him into the web and he was enveloped and entangled, nor could he move hand or foot.

And the boy called out to him and said: O wretched youth, know you that you are entrapped in the web of Zoro the giant magician, and he will return at dusk and take you from the web, then he will ask you your name, and after he will kill you and give your body to me to cook for his supper, for this is his custom. But when he asks your name, say Maqdad, for if your name is Maqdad he will not slay you, rather will he chain you in the manner in which I am chained, and you may escape a dishonourable death to live a miserable life. For Zoro is afraid of none in this world, since it has been revealed to him by his magic book that he will die neither from steel nor from poison, nor have they power over him, but his death will be caused by one named Maqdad, and as for the manner of his death, he knows it not, nor can he discover it. Therefore, if you tell him your name is Maqdad, he will not eat you, being afraid that you may cause him colic or indigestion, resulting in his death. Nor will he slay you, lest your ghost cause him evil, but rather will he chain you here and make you his servant and subject you to his will, that you may do him no harm. My name is Maqdad, therefore he has treated me in this disgraceful manner.

And Maqdad heard the words of the boy and was

75

astonished and he replied: Verily my name is Maqdad. Perhaps I am he who is to cause the death of this tyrant. The boy Maqdad said: But how can this be done? I have caught snakes in this cave, for there are plenty here, and taken their poison and put it in his food, but he laps up the poison like spice. Once when his back was turned, I took the iron spit on which the bodies are cooked and drove it into his heart, even through his body, but he plucked it out and his flesh was as if it had never been pierced, and he caught me and whipped me and thrashed me throughout the night.

The sun set and the world became dark and Maqdad was held in the web in a manner which rendered him powerless. And an evil footstep was heard, and Zoro the Magician was seen to approach. The hearts of the boys were filled with fear, for the body of Zoro was covered in long hair, its colour was green, and it gave off an unholy light. As for his height, it was the height of three men, but he carried his back bent like a hunchback. There was about him the smell of an eater of corpses and the reek of putrefaction, and in his right hand he carried a great whip of which the thong was of dead snakes and from his left hand dangled by their hair two dead children.

And Zoro saw Maqdad entangled in the net and he cried out to him and said: Stranger, what is your name? And Maqdad replied and gave his name truly, nor did he lie. And Zoro's face became creased with rage. He bared his long fangs, shot out his great arms and freed Maqdad from the web with a magic word. Then he carried Maqdad into the cave, and the web parted to let him through. He fastened around Maqdad's neck a collar of iron, and fastened him to the wall with an iron chain, And Maqdad was powerless in the grip of Zoro. Then Zoro drew back and lifted his great whip and said: O bearer of an accursed name, you shall be my servant and you shall be my slave, and should you fail in this I will whip you in this manner. And Zoro lashed Maqdad again and again with the great whip until the clothes were torn from his body and his skin was wet with blood.

Then Zoro threw to the two boys, to both the Maqdads, the bodies of the two children, and he said: Cook them for my supper. And the boys recoiled from the task, but Zoro lashed them with his whip.

Now, behind the wall to which the boys were chained, the rock of the cave was split and there was a passage which grew narrower and narrower until it passed up into the outer air, and it was this passage which served as a chimney to the cave, and at its entrance stood a stand of iron from which hung a large spit. The two boys affixed the bodies of the children to this spit, and they piled underneath them firewood from a heap which lay beside them, and they lit the fire and they roasted the children. Then they brought the food and gave it to Zoro, and he ate of the food and was satisfied. And the boy Maqdad caught two rats, of which there were plenty in the cave, and they cooked the rats and ate them, for they could not bear to eat of the larger dish.

Then Zoro the Magician seated himself at a table and he took from the table a magic book and he set it in front of him and he spoke to it in this fashion: By the power I have over you, O my servant, tell me the truth and answer my questions. And the book answered and replied: I hear and obey you, O my master. And Zoro asked the book: Where shall I find food tomorrow? And the book answered, and its voice was as a woman's voice: In such and such a valley you will find Arabs, and you may slay

77

one of them. And Maqdad was amazed to hear the book speak. Then Zoro asked the book and commanded it: In what manner and in what way shall I meet my death? And the book answered: Verily it shall not be through steel and it shall not be through poison, but your death shall be caused by one named Maqdad and he is now here in this cave. But as to the manner of your death, one greater than I, namely, the Angel of Death, controls this matter and it is forbidden to forecast it.

Then Zoro turned on the two boys and his face was the face of one angered with a terrible anger and he demanded of them: Which of you is he who would cause my death? And Maqdad thought: Escape from this situation will be difficult. Now, Maqdad, when he used to take the sheep to the desert to graze, amused himself and practised at throwing his voice, and in this fashion he could make one sheep talk to another sheep. And he could make any stone or any animal appear to talk to any other stone or animal, yet his lips did not move.

So now Maqdad threw his voice into the chimney, and he answered Zoro and he said: I am he. And Zoro saw that neither of the boys had spoken and the voice came from the chimney and he was amazed. And Zoro turned to the chimney and he said in a terrible voice: What is your name? Who are you? How came you here? And Maqdad threw his voice into the chimney and replied: As for my name, it is Maqdad; as for my station, it is that of a warrior. I came here by magic means, and my mission is to cause your death. And Zoro's fury increased and he commanded: Come out of that chimney. And Maqdad replied: I remain while I wish to remain and I come out when I wish to come out.

Then Zoro went over to the chimney and he thrust in

his hand, but the chimney was long and winding. Then Zoro put his head and shoulders into the chimney and he thrust and thrust with his legs and he propelled himself up the chimney. And he thrust in such a manner that he became firmly fixed in that chimney, and he could move neither forward nor back.

Then the two boys ran to the chimney and Maqdad seized the iron spit and drove it into Zoro, but without result. The younger Maqdad said: We cannot succeed with steel or poison. Let us try fire. And they brought wood and piled it under the chimney and they poured on it oil from the lamp and they lit a great fire under Zoro. And Zoro bellowed in pain and the boys saw that the fire was consuming his flesh.

Then the book spoke out, and its voice was a woman's voice, and it said: I speak freely and not by command out of gratitude for you, O noble Maqdad, who have thus far encompassed the destruction of my master Zoro, and you have removed me from his power by placing fire between me and him. But know, O noble youth, that that fire of yours cannot completely destroy Zoro, and if so much as a hair or fingernail survive from the burning, it will grow during the night into a complete Zoro. But if you place me on the fire I will burn with such a flame that not one evil hair shall survive.

And Maqdad took the book in his hand and said: Lady, for such I believe you to be, before I destroy you, tell me who you are and how you came into this condition. And the book answered and said: My name is Fatima, and I am of the Jann and not of the sons of Adam, but I sinned against their rules and they imprisoned me in this book and laid upon me the duty of obeying him who might possess it. And I came into the possession of this dog, this

79

Zoro, who is half Jinn and half animal, for his father was a Jinn and his mother was a gorilla, and he has some little skill in magic, but of an evil sort. But place me now upon the fire that I may complete the task, and when this book is destroyed, I shall be liberated to return to my race.

And Maqdad placed the book upon the fire and it burnt with an intense blue light, and the body of Zoro was completely consumed. Then the blue light turned into a beautiful girl, who stood beside them, and she said: Thank you, noble Maqdad, for this deed was a pleasant one and it has been of benefit both to the Jann and to the sons of Adam. I would reward you, so command me to do three things before I depart, and you may command me as you desire, and I will obey.

And Maqdad spoke and said: O gentle Lady of the Jann, for the first command, let me and this boy depart in safety from this evil cave. For the second command, let me find my beloved horse, my Rishan, outside and unharmed. And as for the third command, I have never spoken with my father nor have I had that instruction in wisdom and in the art of war which it is the duty of a son to acquire from his father. Let me, lady, have speech with my father.

And the Lady of the Jann spoke and said: Wisely chosen, O boy, for had you asked me for a kingdom or for gold I would have given them to you. But princes are less happy than the rest of men, and gold is only a bringer of jealousy, hatred, and evil. And she levelled her finger at the two boys and the fetters fell from them and the evil web at the mouth of the cave collapsed in dust. And she said: You are free to go and Rishan is outside and unharmed, but you are naked and without money. Go first to that chest and take clothes and gold for your expenses and the arms of your father from the floor. Then leave this cave and mount Rishan and ride in the direction of the north star until the sixth hour of the night. Then shall you see in front of you a fire and a great camp and it will be the camp of your ancestors whom I will bring out from Paradise. For you may not now enter Paradise, since it is written: None shall enter Paradise twice.

So the two boys went to the great chest and opened it and found it filled with clothes and rich stuffs and with gold, and they covered their nakedness with fine clothes and filled their pockets with gold. And Maqdad picked up his father's arms from the floor, and they went out from the cave. And Maqdad saw Rishan standing outside and ran to him and put his arms round his neck and kissed him and said: O my beloved horse, my little Rishan, my heart was sad with longing for you and my eyes were tired with looking for you, for I looked and saw you not.

Then the two boys both mounted Rishan and they rode out and took their course from the north star. And as they rode they passed the time in the pleasures of conversation, and Maqdad said to the boy: Tell me the name of your father, for your name is Maqdad and my name is Maqdad and there will be confusion between us. And the boy answered: My father's name was Ali and he was killed by that tyrant. Now I shall call myself Ibn Ali, and my only desire is to accompany you and be your servant, for you are my liberator.

The two boys rode on into the night in the direction of the north star, until they saw before them a fire and a great camp of black tents of the Arabs, and it was the sixth hour of the night. And a man came out from the camp and walked towards them and the riders saluted the walker and they said: Peace on you. And he replied: And on you peace, and the Mercy of God, and His Blessing. I am Thamir your father, O my son. Enter the guest tent and meet your ancestors. And Maqdad and Ibn Ali entered the guest tent and saluted the assembly.

And there were there seated Degaither and Mansur and Maqdad the son of Degaither and Degaither the son of Mansur and Mansur the son of Qais and Qais the son of Hamed, and Hamed the Lame and Mansur the Father of the Sword, and they all returned the salutations of Maqdad and Ibn Ali and bade them to be seated and they brought for them coffee. And Mansur the Father of the Sword spoke and said: Before the rising of the sun we must fold our tents and load our camels and depart for Paradise. Therefore, draw your sword, O Maqdad, that we may teach you the art of a warrior. Then Maqdad drew his sword and they came at him and taught him the use of the sword. Then he drew his dagger and they taught him to use the dagger. Then he took his mace and they taught him the use of the mace. Then they taught him the use of the spear, and they taught him many tricks which are now forgotten amongst men. Then they taught him how to place troops in battle and how to command an army, and they taught him from their wisdom the entire art of war. And in this manner five hours passed and it was the eleventh hour of night.

Then Thamir said to his son Maqdad: Sleep now, O my beloved son, for you are tired and we also have a journey before us. And they brought blankets and Maqdad and Ibn Ali laid themselves down to sleep in the great guest tent, though first Maqdad embraced and kissed his father and his grandfather and all his ancestors. And Maqdad and Ibn Ali slept for two hours until the sun arose and grew hot and it was the second hour of day. And they then awakened and looked around them, but they could see neither tent nor camp nor Arabs, and they were not covered by blankets. All around them was desert, and only the horse Rishan could be seen. And Maqdad ran to Rishan and kissed him and said: O my little Rishan, we are camped in the desert far from water, and I have caused you suffering.

The two boys mounted Rishan and they rode off, and Maqdad took his course from the sun and rode to the east, that they might come to the river and find water. And after they had ridden for one hour they saw before them a mound, such a mound as is made from the excavated earth from a well, and Maqdad cried: Here is water. And Ibn Ali said: Make haste, let us drink and let the horse drink for we are thirsty. But Maqdad said: Do you not remember, O my comrade, what my ancestors said last night? Namely, that when approaching water you should circle completely around and observe if the camelthorn is broken and if there are tracks for you may find enemies drinking from that water.

So they dismounted and took the horse Rishan and tethered him in a dip in the land, then on foot and in the manner of hunters they circled around the well, and they saw that horses had gone up to it and they had not come out from it, and their track was fresh. Then Maqdad and Ibn Ali crept up to the well, keeping the mound of earth between themselves and the well, and they crept beside the mound and looked at the well, yet they could not be seen. And they saw six horses tethered by the well, and they saw six soldiers, and on the ground lay a seventh horse dead, and the soldiers were pushing and pulling its body towards the well.

And Maqdad whispered to Ibn Ali: These dogs must

83

be Persians, for they mean to drop the body in the well, that the water may become foul, and the raiding Arabs may not drink here. Then Maqdad threw his voice, and he made it come as if from the well and he cried out: Help, help, I am a wealthy merchant drowning in this well. And the six Persians ran to the well and looked down. Then Maqdad and Ibn Ali dashed to the horses, and Maqdad cut the tether ropes with his sword. They each leapt on to a horse, and driving the other horses before them they made off into the desert.

Then Maqdad told Ibn Ali to take the horses far off, and he circled round and returned to the Persians and cried out to them in this manner: O dogs of Persia, know you that we are but scouts of a large raiding party of Arabs which is riding to this well? Now you have no horses and you cannot escape the Angel of Death. Yet I am of a noble and chivalrous nature and I do not like to see the sons of Adam, if indeed such you be, slaughtered in the manner of sheep. Therefore I will give you a chance. Come at me one at a time and if you slay me my friend will cut loose your horses and you may escape from here.

And the Persians discussed amongst themselves and they said: In this there is no difficulty. He is only a beard-less boy. And the bravest of the Persians drew his sword and came towards Maqdad. And Maqdad drew his sword and dismounted and awaited the coming of the Persian. Then the Persian came and struck at Maqdad cunning blows but Maqdad was swift in avoiding the blows of the Persian. And Maqdad fell back before the Persian, and behind him was camelthorn, but he knew it was there for he had first looked to see before the fight started, in the manner taught by his ancestors. As the Persian came forward Maqdad struck at him many blows,

84

and his attention was taken in parrying them and he saw not the camelthorn. His foot caught in its roots and he fell forward, and Maqdad cut off his head.

And the five Persians were shocked to see the death of their comrade at the hands of the beardless boy, but they said: It was but an accident; his foot caught in the root and he fell. Then another Persian drew his sword and came at Maqdad. And Maqdad met him with his sword in his right hand, and in his left hand his headcloth. So they fenced and Maqdad fell back before the Persian. And Maqdad waited until the sun was shining on the face of the Persian, then he struck many blows at the Persian, but he turned them with his sword. And Maqdad waved his headcloth in the air with his left hand, at the same time making with his lips the sound of a sword hissing through the air. For a moment the Persian was deceived and he raised his sword on high to receive the blow, and in that moment Maqdad sliced off his head.

And the four Persians were amazed to see the death of their comrade at the hands of a beardless boy. But they said: Our comrade was a fool. Why did he raise his sword when the boy waved his headcloth? And another Persian came out to fight with Maqdad, but he took his spear and not his sword, for he said: The boy may have some skill with the sword, but what can a youth know of the spear? And Maqdad took up his spear and met the Persian. And the Persian struck many blows at Maqdad, but each time Maqdad slipped aside, and each time he took a pace to the left. And after fighting for some time in this manner, Maqdad dropped his spear on the ground and bent as if to pick it up. And the Persian thought: While the boy is picking up his spear he cannot dodge. So he struck a mighty blow at Maqdad and he put his whole weight behind his spear. But Maqdad did not really pick up his spear from the ground, he only bent and put out his hand. So when the blow came, he leapt aside and seized the spear of the Persian and pulled hard towards himself. And the weight of the Persian was behind that spear, so he fell forward on his face, and Maqdad picked up his spear from the ground and transfixed the Persian before he could rise.

And the three Persians were astonished when they saw the death of their comrade at the hands of the beardless boy, and they whispered amongst themselves and said: Verily, this boy is the Devil himself. And one of them said to the others: Take you the bow, I will go and lure the boy to within bowshot of you, then slay him with an arrow, and in this manner we shall be rid of him and we may go our way. Now, Maqdad was watching the three Persians at the well, for his ancestors had taught him: Watch well your enemies that they may not deceive you. And he saw them whisper and he saw one of them take the bow and he understood their stratagem. So he measured with his eye the distance of a skilful bowshot from the well and he remembered the shape of the camelthorn at that place.

Then the Persian came out and drew his sword and challenged him, and they fought together. And the Persian withdrew before Maqdad and he fell back before him in the direction of his friends. But when they reached the camelthorn which Maqdad had marked, though the Persian fell back Maqdad went no further, nor could he be lured beyond that point. Then when the Persian saw that Maqdad would not follow him he feigned illness and rolled on the ground and made himself appear as a man in agony that Maqdad might come within bowshot. But

Maqdad came not. Rather he took another course, he turned and mounted Rishan, that noble horse, and he took up his great spear and he rode down on the Persian with the speed of the wind, nor could an arrow hit him, and in this manner he speared that Persian and killed him. Then he rode on to the two Persians who stood near the well and he came with such dash and speed that they had no time to draw the bow. And one of them he killed with his spear and the other fell down on the ground before him and begged mercy from him in the most abject manner. And Maqdad commanded the Persian to take off his clothes and the man did so and stood naked before Maqdad.

And Maqdad commanded and said to him: Go to your King, the Shah of the Persians, and enter his presence and salute him, and you shall be in your present naked state. And then shall you say to him: O mighty Shah, look to my condition and see my nakedness, for this shall be the condition of the land of Persia should you desist not from war with the Arabs. For when the men are slain who shall sow the fields? And the land of Persia shall become as barren and naked as I am now. And this is the message of Maqdad son of Thamir, the Arab warrior, and he is from the Fetla tribes. And Maqdad gave the Persian a horse from the six horses, and he mounted and rode off according to the order of Maqdad, nor was he wearing a single stitch of clothing.

Then Maqdad and Ibn Ali watered the horse Rishan, and they continued their journey, taking with them the five horses of the Persians, and their intention was to reach the camp of the tribes. And they rode until the sun was in the west, then they saw the black tents. And they rode up to the greatest tent of all, and it was the guest tent of the

Fetla, and they tethered the horses and entered and saluted the assembly. And seated there were the sheikhs and the warriors of the tribe. They bade them be seated and they brought for them coffee. And the Sheikh spoke to them and said: O strangers who have honoured us, may we know your names, and from whence you come, and from what tribe? And Maqdad replied and answered thus: My tribe is your tribe, for it was the tribe of my father Thamir son of Degaither son of Mansur son of Maqdad son of Degaither son of Mansur son of Qais son of Hamed the Lame son of Mansur the Father of the Sword. But know you I have not before entered amongst you as was fitting, nor have I fought in battle with you, as before I was of tender years, but now I am a man, and I am skilled in the art of war.

And the Sheikhs and the great men of the tribes who were there assembled said: Your name is a known name, for well we remember your father and your grandfather. And out of his great courtesy the Sheikh asked of them concerning their journey, and Maqdad related those events which are known to you, my listeners, nor did he omit any word from the account. And the Sheikh spoke and said: Concerning the magician Zoro, we had information that such a one existed, and we had searched for him, but we did not find him. You have done well to encompass his destruction, for God was with you. But as for these five Persians you say you have killed, know you that boasting is unseemly, and how could a beardless boy do this deed.

And Maqdad looked and he saw disbelief written in the faces of those there present, nor did they believe his words. So he said: Look not at my face, for it is smooth, and neither my moustache nor my beard is grown, but

89

when the farmer sows the seed in the field, perhaps the crop will come early in the year or perhaps it will come late, as is the will of God, and in His time. But know you that I am a man and not a boy, as a sown field is different from the desert, and the crop will come in season. And the Sheikh said: Is your face, then, a field? It is as smooth as the skin of a peach. How, then, can you ride with the warriors in the front of the battle? And Maqdad replied and said: I have slain the Persians and I have taken their horses, and I will challenge the bravest of the Persians to single combat and I will kill him even in front of his Shah, that you may believe my words. And the Sheikh agreed and consented to the words of Maqdad, and a challenge was written and sealed, and a boy took it and delivered it to the camp of the Persians, and it was given and read out to the Shah himself.

And the Shah had heard the words of the naked Persian soldier, as to how the beardless boy had slain five skilled men, and he feared Maqdad, and he ordered the bravest and most skilful Persian soldier to prepare for the combat, and his name was Pahlewan. He had slain more than five hundred men in single combat, and truly his name was feared throughout the land. And a day and an hour was fixed and appointed, and a place was arranged on an island in the River Tigris and the day approached. As for the weapons, the combatants were to use any weapon or method of fighting which they preferred.

And Maqdad ordered Ibn Ali to bring him a shield of Damascus steel, and Ibn Ali executed his command and brought him a shield of the finest steel of Damascus, which was convex in shape like a basin. Then Maqdad ordered Ibn Ali to take out the leather lining of the shield and to burnish the inside until it shone like a mirror, and then he ordered that a leather handle be fixed to the outside of the shield, and Ibn Ali executed the commands of his master. And the shield was prepared and made ready though it presented its inside to an enemy.

The day of the fight dawned, and the army of the Persians gathered on the east bank of the Tigris, and the Arabs of the great tribes came together on the west bank of the Tigris, and a great stand had been erected for the Shah of the Persians and his ladies and his court amongst the Persian troops. In the centre of the river was an island, to this island Maqdad came in a boat from the west bank, and Pahlewan came in a boat from the east bank, and they met on the island. And Maqdad saw that Pahlewan was armed with a great sword the length of which was the height of a man, and Pahlewan came towards Maqdad and his approach was that of a skilful fighter. And Maqdad retreated before Pahlewan, warding off his blows with his sword, and he kept his face to the sun, a position of disadvantage, and Pahlewan was pleased that Maqdad kept his face to the sun and he thought: They were fools who told me that this boy is a skilful fighter. He does not even try to manœuvre to get the sun behind him, and he wears his shield inside out. But at that very moment Maqdad turned his shield towards the face of Pahlewan, and the sun was shining full on the shield, and it was burnished like a mirror and it was concave in shape, for it was reversed, so it concentrated the rays of the sun and flung them fully into the eyes of Pahlewan, and he was forced to close his eyes. And Maqdad ran towards Pahlewan and attacked him, keeping the blinding rays on Pahlewan's eyes. Then Pahlewan struck out with his great sword, but he did not hit Maqdad, and Maqdad cut off Pahlewan's head with a single blow.

And the onlookers were amazed, for they were far off and they did not see how the beardless boy had overcome Pahlewan, and the heart of the Shah of the Persians was full of anger and fear. Then Maqdad turned and shouted across the river to the Persian host, he raised his sword on high and cried: O mighty Shah of Persia, you I will not challenge, for your beard is grey, but you have a son, famous in battle. Send him to me that I may fight him. And the Shah made no reply to Maqdad, but he made a sign signifying that a reply would be sent later, so Maqdad returned to his boat and he crossed the river to the gathering of the tribes.

That night the Shah of Persia held council with his generals and commanders, and the prince his son was present, and a great general spoke and said: Master, it is fitting that the prince your son should fight with the Arab boy, lest the soldiers of our army say he is afraid of a beardless boy, and henceforward they will not follow him in battle, nor will they respect him. And the prince listened and there was fear in his heart. And the Shah ordered the commanders and generals to leave them, and he spoke to his son in this fashion: My son, this Arab boy may not be a great fighter. Perhaps it was luck or some trick of fate which delivered Pahlewan into his hands. It is fitting that you should go and fight him, that your name may be famous as a warrior, and that the soldiers shall fear you. For one day you will be Shah in my place, and if the soldiers and the people of the towns and the peasants do not fear the Shah, then they rise in rebellion and the kingdom is overthrown.

But the prince replied: Father, do not send me out to be slaughtered in the manner of a sheep. This boy is no fighter, he is a magician, and I am unskilled in magic and

92

cannot oppose him. Did you not hear how he slew the five soldiers at the well? Send for a skilled magician that he may destroy the boy, and let me lead my troops into battle as befits a prince. But do not let me be destroyed by some evil power unknown to honest men. But the Shah saw that the face of his son was pale, and he said: I order you to fight this boy, and if you do not then I will kill you with my own hand, and I will beget a son as brave as me to rule Persia when I die. Do you think I am in my tomb? These grey hairs are but a tribute to my learning. I am as vigorous as a man of twenty. I will beget a hundred sons that one of them may come forth a brave man. A coward shall not wrap me in my shroud nor shall a craven inherit my throne.

The prince, the son of the Shah of Persia, returned to his tent and his heart was filled with a great sadness. He took up his mirror and looked at his face and it was beautiful to behold, so he said: O noble eyes, dignified as the eyes of a hawk, O lofty brow, O brave moustache, O sweet red lips to which the girls of Isfahan have written verses, shall you then rot and decay, hidden forever in the tomb from the eyes of men? Or shall I flee and hide this noble face forever from the gaze of men of honour? I cannot fight this boy, for my heart is filled with fear and my hand is shaking. And the prince commenced weeping and his sobs would have wrung the heart of a listener.

And his sister, for the prince had a sister of his own age whom he loved, heard his sobs and came to him in the tent. And he related to his sister, the beloved Princess Jamila, the words of his father the Shah. And the princess grieved much at the words of her brother and said: Should you fight this boy, then without doubt you will be killed, for they say in the camp that he has greater skill than anyone in our army or in the whole of Persia. And should you defy our father, then he will surely slay you, and should you flee, then how will you live in a strange land, since you know no trade and no occupation? There is only one way and one course open which promises success, and that is that I should fight this boy in your place.

And the prince looked at his sister sadly, for he thought that God had deprived her of her reason, but she continued, saying: We are of one face and we are as alike as two matches in a box, save that you have a moustache and my face is smooth. But I will make myself a moustache of sheep's wool and glue it to my lip, and when I go out to do battle with the boy our father will not know me from you. But whereas, if you fight the boy you will be slain, yet I have a woman's wit and a woman's weapons, and know you that my body is so beautiful that no man can gaze on it and retain his reason. And I will wear such a cloak that I can open it from the front, and beneath it I will wear no shirt or other garment, so that when we are fighting I can slip back the cloak. When he is stunned by what he sees, I shall slay him before he can recover. Yet the armies on the banks of the river will not be able to see what has happened. However, you must shave off your moustache and take your place with the women on that day. For, were our father to see me absent, he would ask where I was, and our ruse might be discovered.

And the prince replied: It is as you say. We have one face since we are begotten by the same father from the same mother, and your idea may save the land of Persia from being deprived of an heir to the throne. So the prince went to his father and he said: Send a messenger to the camp of the Arabs and tell them that the prince will fight. And the heart of the Shah was filled with joy at the courage of his son.

The day of combat dawned, and the army of the Persians gathered on the east bank of the Tigris and the Arabs of the great tribes collected on the west bank. And the Princess Jamila was wearing a man's cloak and a shield and a sword, and to her face was affixed a moustache of sheep's wool, and all who saw her thought she was the prince. And as for the prince, he had shaved off his moustache and was wearing the dress of a girl, and he was seated with the royal ladies, and all who saw him thought that he was the Princess Jamila.

The Princess Jamila got into a boat and was taken out to the island in the middle of the Tigris, and Maqdad came in a boat from the west bank. And the Princess met Maqdad on the island, and she told him to send back his boat to the bank, and she returned her own boat to the bank, speaking in the voice of a man. And Maqdad, when he saw that the Persian boat was returning to the shore, ordered his own boat back. So Maqdad and the Princess were left alone on the island and those on the banks of the river could only see them from afar. But Maqdad thought the Princess was a man, heir to the throne of Persia.

The Princess made a sign to Maqdad that the fight was to begin. She drew her sword and Maqdad drew his sword and they came together. As their swords met Maqdad saw that the wrist of his enemy was weak, and he thought: This prince is no fighter. I can slay him when I desire to slay him. But rather should I disarm him and take him back captive, that we may collect his ransom and force his father to accept our terms.

So he played and fenced with his adversary, nor did he strike a fatal blow. And as they were fencing thus the

95

Princess put her left hand to her cloak and undid the knot and she pulled back her cloak. Then Maqdad saw that the prince had the body of a most beautiful woman and he was struck with astonishment. He dropped his sword to the ground and stepped back and said: O lady, for such you appear to me to be, had I known that you were to fight me then had I prepared another weapon, for the sword must not spoil such beauty. And the Princess advanced on Maqdad with her sword upraised to strike the blow of death. But her heart was a woman's heart and she saw that Maqdad was handsome of the face and she did not strike the blow. And tears came to her eyes and Maqdad took her sword from her hand and he called for his boat, crying: The Persian prince is my prisoner. And Maqdad put her in the boat and they returned to the Arab shore. And the Shah and the Persians and the Arabs on the banks of the river were stricken with astonishment, for they had not seen what Maqdad had seen, and the Shah said: This was magic, for the Arab boy was disarmed and without a sword. Yet my son surrendered to him.

And Maqdad took the Princess Jamila to his tent and she related to him what had passed between her and her brother, and Maqdad was filled with an exceeding love for the Princess and he meditated to find a way of marrying her without disgracing her or her brother. And as for the Persian prince, he sat amongst the ladies and his heart was filled with fear, and he thought: How long am I to remain a woman? This disgrace is greater than if I had fled through cowardice. What will happen when my father marries me to some prince?

And Maqdad told nobody that the Persian prince was a woman, and he kept her captive in his tent, and he wrote a letter to the Shah and he wrote:

H

O Majesty the Shah, after the most respectful salutations I write to inform you that I am engaged in praying for Your Majesty's health, and as for your son the Prince, let it be known to you that he is in good health and he is my guest, and he occupies his time in praying for Your Majesty's health. And it would be fitting if the request which I am now about to lay at Your Majesty's feet were made by one of my friends or relations but in the present condition of war courtesy must fall by the way. And my request is this, that you give me your daughter the Princess Jamila in marriage, and if you name a price, that price will be paid, and as for her dowry, let her bring a pomegranate seed. My name is a known name and my pedigree is a known pedigree, and it is desirable that you send the Princess in a boat, as, due to the state of war, I cannot come to you. And let the Prince your son be present at the celebration of the marriage, and after it is concluded, even the duty of hospitality shall not cause us to detain him further. So he will return to your camp in safety and in peace.

And Maqdad signed and sealed the letter and sent it to the Persian camp.

The Shah of the Persians opened the letter of Maqdad and read it, and his face became black with anger and rage and he bellowed a bellow and roared a roar and he sent for his generals and his ministers and he shouted: This son of a camel has captured my son and now he wants to marry my daughter. And he ordered his generals to prepare a plan for attacking the camp of the tribes and rescuing his son and killing Maqdad. But the generals looked grave and they said: Master, how can this be? It is true that our army is ten times the size of the force of these Arab tribesmen, but when we march against them they fade away as do the bats at the first rays of the morning sun. But they return when we least expect them and kill our men and drive off our animals and they are gone before our army is in battle array.

And one of the generals spoke and said: Master, might it not be political and diplomatic to give your daughter to this boy? For he is truly a great warrior and it were better that he be our friend than our enemy, and as for his pedigree, it is as he says, for in no royal house can you find a pedigree which equals that of the simplest Arab tribesman. But the Shah said: This cannot and shall not be. Either you, my commanders, evolve a plan to secure the release of my son or I will have you roped between horses and torn apart. And meanwhile I will marry my daughter to a prince of Turkey, that no man who calls a host his father, no product of love in a ditch, shall come to me and insult me by asking for her in marriage. Send now for my daughter that I inform her of my decision.

A page went from the tent of the Shah to the women's quarter, and he spoke to the eunuch on guard and said: Tell the Princess Jamila that the Shah her father commands her presence, for he is arranging her marriage to a prince of Turkey. And the eunuch delivered the message to the Prince, who was dressed as the Princess Jamila, and he said: Mistress, your father commands your presence, for he is arranging your marriage to a prince of Turkey. And the face of the Prince went pale with fear, for he thought: Now what will happen when the Turkish prince comes in to me on the night of the wedding? And he could see no escape from his misfortune.

So the Prince, wearing the veil and dress of a lady, went into the presence of his father the Shah. And the Shah spoke and said: Beloved daughter, your interest touches my heart, and let it be known to you that some months ago the noble Prince Jalal of Turkey sent to us an ambassador and requested that I give you him in marriage. But seeking your advantage, and to advance affairs of state, I delayed answer, and I sought a better match. But you are now too old to remain long unmarried, for you are in the seventeenth year of your life. I am therefore sending an embassy of great dignity and magnificence to the noble Prince, and my ambassador will carry my acceptance of the Prince's offer. He will start on the morrow, with an escort of a thousand horsemen and a thousand footmen, and he will take with him one hundred slave girls of great beauty from Kafkaz as a present to the Sultan. But the Prince, speaking with the voice of a girl, said: O my father, do not marry me to this prince, this horrible Turk; marry me rather to the Arab boy, Maqdad, for him I love for his courage and the mercy he showed my brother, when he had overcome him by magic.

The Shah said: The decision is made and the execution awaits accomplishment, but your voice is strange today, O my little darling daughter. And the Prince replied: When my heart is broken shall not my voice break?

Then the Shah ordered the Commander of the Eunuchs to come into his presence, and he commanded him, saying: Take the Lady Jamila back to her tent, and search that tent for any knife or anything sharp enough to cut a vein and search it for poison, and search all who come into her presence. For she is full of the foolishness of youth and she desires not her marriage, and she may take her life. Put upon her tent a guard of ten eunuchs, and watch her that she escapes not, for if she dies or escapes us, then torture awaits you, and you will lose your eyes and your tongue even as you have been deprived in other ways.

And the Commander of the Eunuchs answered: Master, she shall not escape, either in death or in life.

The Commander of the Eunuchs took the Prince back to the tent of the Princess his sister, and he searched the tent and he found the razor which the Prince used to keep his face as smooth as a girl's, and the Commander of the Eunuchs said: O my mistress, so you had already sent for a razor to cut your vein. And the heart of the Prince was cold with fear, for he thought: Without that razor my moustache will grow and my fate will be sealed. The Commander of the Eunuchs placed a guard of ten eunuchs of great stature, armed with swords, upon that tent.

Then the Prince, using the voice of the Princess, called for a slave girl whom he knew to be devoted to his sister and she came to the tent, and she was searched by the eunuchs for weapons and for poison, but they found that she had none with her, and they permitted her to enter. And the Prince, using the voice of a girl, said to the slave girl: O my eyes, know you that I love the boy Maqdad and I will not marry this Turk. Listen well and take this message to the Commander of the Cavalry, for he is in fear of his life should he not rescue my brother, and he will help me in this to save himself. Tell him that the Lady Jamila sends him this message:

Know you that through a trick, and by applying a moustache of sheep's wool to my face, I will at dawn tomorrow appear in the guise of my brother the Prince, now a captive in the Arab camp. Seize tonight the Court Magician and threaten him with death if he does not tell my father the Shah that through magic the boy Maqdad has taken me, the Lady Jamila, from my tent in the night without the guards being aware of it, and he has left in my place my brother the Prince. And let him keep this a secret from everyone else in the camp and in the world. Then when my father knows that his daughter is in Maqdad's hands he will consent to the match from very shame, for should this become known in the world, then the Turkish prince would never marry me and our family will be disgraced. Advise my father that though I am a man and the Prince his son, I should dress as a girl, as the lady my sister, and he should send me over to the Arab camp to marry Maqdad, and when I am there I shall stay only to return as myself the Prince. Though in very fact and unknown to my father I will marry Maqdad and the Prince my brother will be released.

And the slave girl said: O my beloved mistress, this is indeed a clever scheme, but how can you pass as a man? And the Prince, in the voice of the Princess, replied: I shall pass as my brother and my father will not know the difference, for we are of one face and we are as alike as two matches in a box, save for the moustache which I shall affix to my face tomorrow. But go you now and deliver the message. Then bring to me under your clothes a man's clothes, but wear them, so that when the eunuchs search and feel your body for knives and bottles of poison they may not detect them. And the slave girl went and she gave the message to the Commander of the Cavalry and she brought back the clothes to the tent.

The Commander of the Cavalry heard the message given him by the slave girl and he was astonished at what he heard. He thought: My master the Shah will become as mad as a camel at the time of mating when he hears that the Princess Jamila has been taken in the night by magic and the Prince her brother left in her place. But he cannot in justice blame the affair on me, and should he believe that this has really taken place, then he cannot kill us, his commanders, for failing to rescue the Prince, for the Prince will be safe in our camp. And as for the Princess, what will be the point of rescuing the Princess after she has been taken to this Arab's tent? But the danger is great. Can the Lady Jamila pass as her brother? But he decided: A danger and a risk is better than certain death, for how can I rescue the Prince from the Arab camp?

The Commander of the Cavalry sent for the Court Magician, and he came and entered his tent and saluted him. And the Commander spoke in this fashion: You know how quickly my sword comes from its scabbard and how truly it strikes. From now until dawn you will remain in my tent, closely guarded, and at dawn you and I will go to the tent of our Master the Shah, and we will wake him and then you will say to him: O master, I was looking in my magic glass in the night, and I saw a cat come into our camp and go into the tent of our mistress, the Lady Jamila. And in the mouth of the cat was a rat, and the cat laid the rat upon the bed of our mistress and I knew from my magic power that the cat was Maqdad, the Arab magician, and the rat was our master the Prince. I tried to say a spell, but I was held by some terrible power, for verily this Maqdad is a prince of magicians.

Then the cat spat into the face of our lady Mistress, and she also turned into a rat, and the cat took her in his mouth and went out from the tent and from the camp.

And when the cat had crossed the river and there was water between me and him, I was released from the spell which held me, and I turned to my magic books, and after working for two hours I worked a spell which turned our master, His Highness the Prince, back into his former state, and he is now lying sleeping in the tent of the lady his sister, and I have told nobody of this affair save His

103

Excellency the Commander of your Cavalry, for he is verily the most discreet and ablest of your officers. And when you say this to the Shah I shall be standing behind you and my hand will be on my sword, and should you vary one word of it I will strike you dead, crying: A plot to kill Your Majesty.

The Court Magician was filled with fear, and he said: But how can the Shah believe these words? For will he not go straight to the tent of our lady the Princess, and there he will find her sleeping. It is said she is closely guarded, while the Prince is indeed a prisoner in the Arab camp? But the Commander of the Cavalry said: Our lady the Princess will disguise herself as the Prince her brother, for they are of one face. Only she will fasten a moustache of sheep's wool to her face. And I will then advise the Shah to agree to the marriage with the boy Maqdad, and I will advise him to disguise his son the Prince as the lady Princess, that he may send her over in state and dignity for the marriage. And that the Prince is really the Princess the Shah will know not. And the boy Maqdad will agree to this trick to save his wife from shame. The Court Magician liked not the words of the Commander of the Cavalry, but he saw his sword and he consented.

At the first light of dawn the Commander of the Cavalry and the Court Magician went to the tent of the Shah, and they passed the guards and they wakened the Shah and the Commander of the Cavalry said: Master, your son the Prince is returned and sleeping safely in the tent of the Lady Jamila, but the Lady Jamila has been taken to the Arab camp. And the Court Magician said the words which had been told him by the Commander of the Cavalry, nor did he alter a single word of it, for the hand of the Commander of the Cavalry was on his sword.

Then truly the Shah became as mad as a camel at the time of mating, and he rose from his bed in his tent and ran to the tent of his daughter, and the Commander of the Cavalry and the Court Magician followed him, and they passed the eunuchs and entered the tent. And they saw lying on the bed a figure wearing man's clothes and with a moustache. And as for the Commander of the Cavalry and the Court Magician, they thought the figure to be that of the Princess Jamila disguised as her brother, and as for the Shah, the figure appeared to be that of the Prince his son, brought in the night from the Arab camp. And as for you, my listeners, you know that the figure was indeed the figure of His Highness the Prince, though he had laid aside the clothes of a woman, and had put on the clothes of a man, and he had put on a moustache of sheep's wool, for his own moustache was only one day grown. And though the Shah was frothing at the mouth like a mad dog and pacing the tent like a courting bustard, his brain still worked and he thought: Perchance this is some trick of the Princess Jamila to escape to her lover, perhaps she has bribed the Court Magician and put on a false moustache that she may escape from this tent. So the Shah commanded: Wake him.

The Commander of the Cavalry wakened the sleeping Prince, and the Prince opened his eyes and said: I marvel at this state of affairs. I went to sleep a guarded prisoner in the Arab camp and I awake in the tent of my sister in our own camp, and you my father are present to greet me. But the Shah commanded: Pull that moustache and pull it hard. And the Commander of the Cavalry advanced to execute the Shah's order. And the hearts of the Commander of the Cavalry and the Court Magician were full of fear. And the Commander thought: How can I pull this moustache hard without it coming off, and the smooth face of our Lady the Princess be shown? And the Prince was also fearful, for the moustache was indeed false. So he said: Father, do not let my moustache be pulled, for does not the proverb say: A man's honour is in the hair of his moustache. If you want to know if I am man or woman, for such appears to be your object, let me prove my sex in another way. Go you from this tent and send into it a slave girl, one whom you trust, and you may choose any girl you like in this camp, and let her come into me. Then let her come out and testify that I am a man.

And the Shah agreed, and he sent for a personal slave girl whom he trusted, and he and the Commander of the Cavalry and the Court Magician stood outside the tent. And the Shah ordered the slave girl: Enter the tent, and when you come out you shall testify whether the person within it is a man or a woman. And the slave girl entered the tent and the legs of the Commander of the Cavalry and the Court Magician were trembling through very fear, for they thought that their plot was discovered.

The slave girl came out from the tent and she said: I testify by the most solemn oath that the Prince within the tent is a man and not a woman. And the Shah believed her words. And as for the Commander of the Cavalry and the Court Magician, both of them were astonished. And they thought: How did the Princess, our mistress, work this trick?

Then the Shah and the Commander of the Cavalry and the Court Magician entered the tent, and the Shah was convinced that his daughter had indeed been taken in the night by magic. And the Commander of the Cavalry spoke and said: Master, this event is only known to us in this tent and to the Arab boy, and to no other in the world, and the secret can be preserved. Let the Prince here dress as his sister and send him over in all state and dignity to marry the Arab. The Arab boy will be satisfied, for he will in fact marry the Princess, whether we like it or not, and it will not be known in the world that the sanctity of your harem was violated.

And the Shah agreed and commanded the Prince: I will send you a razor and a woman's dress. Make your face as smooth as a girl's face and dress in your sister's clothes. Then nobody can tell you from her. Then shall I send you over to the Arab camp in state and you will go to the tent in which your sister now is, though the world thinks you are yourself a captive in it. Then shall you change to a man's dress, and Maqdad may marry your sister in accordance with custom and religion.

But the Prince said: Father, I cannot dress as a girl. This will be a great shame for me. But the Shah commanded him and said: The order is given.

Then the Shah and the Commander of Cavalry and the Court Magician returned to the Shah's own tent. And as they went the Commander of the Cavalry whispered to the Shah: Master, the Court Magician knows that your daughter was abducted in the night, and a secret is less secret the more it is shared. And the Shah whispered back: You are right. Kill him. Then the Commander of the Cavalry whipped out his sword and killed the Court Magician with a single blow, before he could utter a single word. And the Commander of the Cavalry went to the Shah's tent with the Shah, and the Shah commanded him: Leave your sword outside my tent, for it smells of blood. And the Commander of the Cavalry obeyed the order of his master the Shah. And when they had entered the tent and the door was closed, the Shah took up his own sword and said: You spoke truly when you said that a secret shared is no secret, and you also know this secret. And the Shah killed the Commander of his Cavalry with a single blow, and he was without a weapon with which to defend himself.

Then the Shah took a woman's clothes and a razor and he returned to the Prince, and he said: Make yourself as a girl. Then the Shah went out of the tent and he called for pages and ordered them to awaken the camp and to assemble the court, and the trumpets sounded and the wazirs and great men and commanders and generals came into the presence of the Shah.

And the Shah spoke and said: Know you that I have decided to give my beloved daughter, the Princess Jamila, to the noble and brave Arab boy, Maqdad the son of Thamir, of the Fetla tribes. And her dowry shall be one hundred thousand liras in gold and a thousand horses and a thousand riding camels, and as for the price which I shall ask of the boy, it shall be a water melon. And owing to the state of war I shall send her and her dowry in boats across the river, starting in one hour from now. Send messengers to the boy Maqdad that he may be apprised of these facts. But the wazirs and commanders looked grave and they spoke and said: Master, to you is the ordering and to us is obedience, but we had hoped for a better match for your daughter. And the Shah spoke and said: The pedigree of the simplest Arab tribesman is better than that of the noblest prince, and courage in battle is better than wide domains. So messengers went out and the orders of the Shah were carried out.

And when Maqdad heard the news his heart was full of joy, for though the Princess was in his tent, he did not know how to marry her without destroying her honour

108

and the honour of her brother. And the Prince came across the river dressed as the Princess, and they took him to the tent in which was the Princess dressed as the Prince, and there, alone and unseen, they changed their clothes and became their proper selves.

Then Maqdad married the Princess and loved her with an exceeding love and had many sons as brave as their ancestors, and the Prince returned across the river to his father the Shah, and when his father died he ruled Persia in his place, and all who saw him thought that he was a lion in courage, nor was there any revolt among his subjects, and in the whole world only he and Maqdad and the Lady Jamila knew that he had been afraid to fight a beardless boy and that he had dressed as his sister to avoid the fight.

A MAN'S HONOUR IS IN THE

HAIR OF HIS MOUSTACHE

On the morning after the night in which we had heard the story of Maqdad, we halted for breakfast near Mussayib. Hamed said: You heard the story of Maqdad and you heard how the Persian Prince said that a man's honour is in the hair of his moustache. Now this is a true proverb of the Fetla tribes and I will relate how this saying originated, though truly the Prince was a man without honour, for he shaved off his moustache. And Abed said: If you know the true facts of the origin of this proverb, then tell us the story.

AND Hamed related:

Once in Hilla there was a cloth merchant of moderate wealth, and his name was Abdul Rashid Mejid. This merchant used to buy cloth from the great merchants of Baghdad and he used to sell it in small quantities to the tribesmen and the people of Hilla. He made no great profit from his shop, but he had enough money for the rent of his house and for his food. He kept no servants in his house, for the work of the house was done by his wife and by his only daughter, a girl of great beauty, in the sixteenth year of her life. The name of the girl was Salma.

And one day it happened that at the hour of noon the hub in their house was empty of water, and the mother of Salma said to her: Go to the river and bring water for the hub. And Salma put a jar on her shoulder and she went to the river. But it was her habit not to go to that part of the river which ran through the town and was near to her house, for she was ashamed that she, a daughter of a merchant, should be seen drawing water, for the women who drew water were the wives and daughters of the porters, and the fellahin, and the leather workers and the coppersmiths, but the daughters of the cloth merchants used to have servants to draw water. Yet her father would have no servant, for his trade was not great. So she went out of the back of her house through the palm trees to a secluded part of the river.

When Salma reached the river she was hot and tired, for the time was noon and the season was summer. She looked around her, but she could see not a single living soul, nor was there a sound from the bazaar or from the town, for the whole world was sleeping. So she thought: I will cool and refresh myself before I return to the house.

She took off her clothes and put them on the bank, and she stepped into the river. Now, be it known to you that, though she could see him not, there was concealed on the bank a youth of the Fetla tribes, and his name was Kadhim. He did not own a single horse or mare, nor did he even own the leg of a mare. He owned no sheep and he owned no land, and he lived by eating at the guest tent of his sheikh. And as for clothes, he used to go to the river and set snares for the sandgrouse and partridges when they came to drink, and sell them in the market to buy cloth.

And Kadhim was concealed on the bank of the river watching his snares when he saw a girl beautiful as a moon come to the river and divest herself of her clothes. He saw that she was perfect in figure, for her neck was slender and her shoulders smooth and soft and her breasts rose firmly and clearly as do the desert dunes in moonlight. As for her waist it was slender and her thighs were round and smooth and around her navel was tattooed a butterfly. And he watched her and forgot the sandgrouse and he forgot the partridges. And after she had bathed in the river she dried herself by lying in the sun. Then she put on her clothes and filled the jar with water and returned to the town.

And the next day at the rising of the sun Kadhim concealed himself in the same place and awaited the coming of the girl. And about half an hour after dawn she came down and drew water from that very same place. And Kadhim, who was concealed in the tamarisk bushes, watched her, but she did not take off her clothes. She merely filled the pot with water and put it on her shoulder, and she turned and returned to the town. But Kadhim, who was a youth in the seventeenth year of his life and swift of foot, ran ahead behind the fruit groves and date trees and came out on the path ahead of her, and when

112

1

she drew near he greeted her and wished her the peace of God and His blessing. And Salma drew her veil across her face and she averted her eyes and she did not reply to the greeting of the strange youth. Then Kadhim drew level with her and he bent his head towards her and whispered: Did it hurt much when they tattooed the butterfly? When Salma heard these words her face grew red with shame. But she looked at Kadhim's face and saw that he was laughing, so she, too, laughed, and she dropped her veil and said: Since you have seen the butterfly you may as well see my face.

Then Kadhim and Salma sat down by a tamarisk bush, and he told her his name and situation and she told him her name and details of her life, and they laughed much about the butterfly and she said: It did not hurt, for it was done when I was in the fifth year of my life, and it was only a little one, but it has grown larger with me. And they discovered that they were of one heart.

Each day and every day that Salma went to draw water from the river Kadhim waited for her, and he helped her fill the jar with water, and they would sit down by a tamarisk bush and pass a few minutes in laughter and happiness. And when Salma returned to her house her eyes were like stars and her cheeks were like the blossoms of the rose. And the mother of Salma said to her husband, the merchant Abdul Rashid: See how happy our daughter is? What can cause this happiness? And Abdul Rashid said: She needs a husband. Perhaps she is falling in love. I will see the marriage broker today.

So that very day, when he had closed his shop, Abdul Rashid went to the house of that discreet man, the marriage broker, and he said: My daughter is of an age to marry. And the broker said: There is one who seeks a

114

bride of fifteen or sixteen years, and he is Abbas Ali el Qassab, that wealthy merchant. His shop is said to be worth three thousand gold liras. And the matter was discussed and the broker passed much between the two merchants, and all was ready for a formal proposal. And Abdul Rashid Mejid said: First I will ask the mother of the girl and the girl, for this matter affects them. Then let matters take a formal course.

Abdul Rashid Mejid went back to his house, and his daughter and his wife brought him food. And when he had eaten of the food he said: There is good news for our little Salma. I will arrange for her to marry Abbas Ali el Qassab, so that she can live in a fine house and have servants of her own, nor shall she have to draw water or soil her hands with cooking, and she will be too grand to come and see her poor parents.

But Salma started crying and sobbing and she said: Abbas Ali has no front teeth and he dyes his beard and water runs always from his nose in the manner that it drips from the fronds of the palm trees when it rains. And she flung herself on the ground and her body was racked with sobs. And her mother said to her father: Don't worry, I will talk her round. I was like this when they told me I had to marry you.

Next morning at dawn Salma ran to the river and Kadhim took her in his arms, for she was sobbing and trembling like a tent in the wind. And she related to Kadhim what had passed between her and her father. And he asked: What price does your father want for you? And she replied: Eighty gold liras.

Then Kadhim said to the girl Salma: Do not weep and do not fear, for on the day that Abbas Ali el Qassab puts on his sword and mounts his horse to ride in procession to your father's house, on that day shall I introduce him to the Angel of Death. And Salma said: Only take me away with you to your tribe, that I may be safe from evil. Kadhim replied: You have seen our camps and our villages, and you have seen how the walls of the houses are of mud bricks, and the roofs are of the cloth of our tents or of straw matting. But do you know the reason for this? We of the tribes do not close both our eyes when we sleep. Perhaps the Turks will impose an unjust tax on us, or perhaps a Turkish soldier will speak to one of our women and he will die, or perhaps someone will seek refuge with us and the Turks will command us to sur-render him. Then will our Sheikh cry: Sheil, and in less time than it takes to snuff a candle we are gone into the desert with our camels and horses and sheep, and all our property, even to the roofs of our houses, is loaded on our camels and is gone away. And when the Turkish troops arrive they find only the empty mud walls of our houses, which they cannot burn. And they find our crops sown in the field and they find our palm trees, and they may destroy some of them, and they try to seek us in the desert, but they cannot find us. And then we will ride against the Turks and we will destroy their caravans on the road to Basra and we will destroy their boats on the river, until the Turkish Governor cries: Do not pay the tax, or, Do not surrender the fugitive. But you are used to an easier life, for you should have a house and servants of your own, and you should not have to drink the water from a camel's stomach. I will marry you, but first I mean to become a great merchant, that I may give you a house and brass cooking-pots and a servant and two anklets of silver and a bangle of gold.

Salma left Kadhim and returned to the town, and there

was no fear in her heart, for she knew that Abbas Ali el Qassab would die before he could marry her. And Kadhim sat watching his snares and thinking: How can I become a great merchant? Kadhim was so poor that he had not even a single copper coin in his pocket; he owned no shoes, he had no headcloth, he was not even wearing any vest or underclothes, and his only garment was his thob. And Kadhim decided: I will borrow money, and trade with my capital and become a great merchant.

Then Kadhim went to the town and he was walking in his bare feet, and he went to the shop of Abdul Rashid and saluted the merchant and said: Give me a roll of cloth and a loan of five gold liras and I will give you my pledge. And Abdul Rashid looked and he saw that the youth was dressed in a dirty and torn thob and that he was bareheaded and barefooted, but he saw that he carried his head like a hawk, so he said: You are, then, from the tribes? And Kadhim nodded and said: Yes.

Now, let it be known to you that the tribes were much poorer in the days of the Ottomans than they are today, for they were then unable to cultivate their land in peace and prosperity, and it often happened that it was necessary to celebrate a marriage or observe the rites of death when there was no money in the purse of the head of the house. Then would he go to the town and to a merchant and say: Give me cloth and money and take my pledge. And as for the pledge, if he had a gold or silver ring, he would give it, and if he had none then he would give his headcloth to the merchant, or even his riding switch, saying: This contains my honour. And when the pledge was given payment was always made, for this is the custom of the tribes.

Abdul Rashid Mejid looked at the youth Kadhim and

he saw that he was truly from the tribes, for his bearing was proud and his gaze the gaze of the peregrine falcon. So he said: Take the money and the cloth and give me your pledge. Then Kadhim's cheeks flushed red, for he had forgotten to bring a pledge with him, nor did he own a ring, and he had no headcloth and he owned no riding switch, for he had no horse. But his brain was quick and he thought and answered: Verily a man's honour is contained in the hair of his moustache, for it is his moustache that distinguishes his face from that of a woman or a boy. Therefore I shall give you one hair of my moustache as a pledge. And Abdul Rashid Mejid was astonished at the words of the youth.

Then Kadhim called for scissors and for a mirror, and he studied his face in the mirror and searched for a hair in his moustache which was less beautiful than the rest. And he found such a hair and snipped it off and gave it to Abdul Rashid Mejid. And Abdul Rashid Mejid took the hair and put it with the pledges, and he put it in a box with the rings and the headcloths and riding switches, and he gave Kadhim five gold liras and a roll of cloth.

Kadhim took the money and the cloth and he went to the shop of a tailor whom he knew and trusted, for the man's father was from the Fetla tribes. He said to the tailor: Take this cloth and this money and make me the clothes of a very rich merchant, and bring me a beard of sheep's wool which I will fasten to my face, and keep this a secret, for it is more important to me than life itself. And the tailor said: Cut my head to keep the secret. Then the tailor made for Kadhim the clothes of a wealthy merchant and he brought for him a beard of sheep's wool, and when Kadhim had put on the beard and put on the clothes he looked so important and distinguished that anyone who saw him would say: This is a merchant whose shop is worth ten thousand gold liras.

Kadhim, dressed as a wealthy merchant, went out from the shop of the tailor and he returned to the shop of Abdul Rashid Mejid. He entered the shop and greeted Abdul Rashid Mejid and wished him the peace of God. And Abdul Rashid Mejid rose when he saw the wealthy merchant enter his shop, and he returned his greeting, and he ordered the shop boy to bring a glass of tea from the coffee house for the distinguished visitor. And Kadhim sat in the chair which Abdul Rashid Mejid placed for him.

Now, Kadhim, though a simple tribal boy, had travelled as far as Basra with the Sheikh, for in ancient times when the Sheikh travelled to Baghdad or to Basra he took fifty men in his retinue, that all who saw him might recognise his dignity and position and, as Kadhim had no land and no sheep, he used to accompany the Sheikh and eat at his expense in the hotels of Basra. So he had some knowledge of affairs.

Kadhim drank the glass of tea in the shop of Abdul Rashid Mejid and he asked after the health of his host. He said: Know you that I am a merchant of Basra and my trade is a general trade, and I deal in every article and every commodity, for my firm is a great firm with branches in India and in Persia and in Nejd. And let it be known to you that I have come to Hilla to seek a merchant of honesty and repute to act as my agent that I may transact various kinds of business at this place. So I asked from the great merchants and bankers of Baghdad that they give me the names of those merchants at Hilla who are reliable in their dealings, and they told me the name of your honour and of his honour our brother Abbas Ali el Qassab. But they said of the last named that water drips from his nose as it does from the fronds of the palm trees when it rains and that he dyes his beard, but grey hairs honour a man, and a man who would falsify his beard might well falsify the accounts. Therefore I have come to your honour with my request.

Abdul Rashid Mejid was overjoyed at the words of the wealthy merchant, and he thought: I did not know that the great merchants of Baghdad even knew my name, yet they know of me and know that I am honest. This is indeed a reward for my many years of honest if simple trade. And how great is the knowledge and command of affairs of these mighty merchants, that they even know that Abbas Ali el Qassab dyes his beard and that his nose drips as do the palm fronds in rain. And the heart of Abdul Rashid was full of gladness that he at last had the chance to engage in great commerce. So he said: I am willing to do anything you wish and your commands will be dearer to me than my eyes. But please may I know your name?

Kadhim, in the guise of the wealthy merchant, replied: Forgive me, I had thought you had recognised my face, for it is a known face in the bazaars of Baghdad, Basra, Mosul and India. My name is Abdul Hamed el Atraqchi and my address is in the city of Basra in the bazaar of Umm el Brum at the Khan of the Indian, and there I may be found. For Kadhim knew it would take a fortnight for a letter to travel to Basra and a fortnight for an answer to return. Abdul Rashid Mejid did not recognise the name of Abdul Hamed el Atraqchi, but he thought: I must not show myself a yokel in front of this distinguished man. So he said: Your name is a known name and I am honoured that you should visit me. But what, sir, is your business?

Kadhim replied: Please keep my presence here the closest secret, for were the traders to hear my name and to know that I am here to buy, prices would rise a hundredfold. But know you that I am here to buy a thousand horses and a thousand mares of the finest Arab stock and I am going to take them to Basra, where the prices are very high, for they can be from there shipped to India, where the British officers are fighting the Hindus and the Sikhs and conquering the country, and they will pay huge prices for a good horse or mare. And what I require of you is that you do the buying, for I cannot show my face in the horse market without raising the prices. Then when I have the horses I will take them to Basra and send you a draft on Baghdad and I will share the profits with you half and half.

Abdul Rashid thought and spoke: I know that the price of horses is much higher at Basra than at Hilla, but how many of the horses will reach Basra, for you have to traverse the territory of the great tribes, and indeed the tribesmen love horses, and if they do not come on you in the day and take them by force, they will come on you at night at your camp and take what they will by stealth.

Kadhim answered, and his answer was firm and dignified: I will take the risk, for though you shall be my partner in the profit, I alone shall bear the loss, for what will these two thousand horses cost us? Not much more than twenty thousand gold liras, I think. Why, I have lost or won a larger amount in a single night at gambling.

Abdul Rashid Mejid was much impressed by the words of the wealthy merchant and he thought: If the horses get through to Basra then the profit will truly be enormous, but if they are lost or stolen on the road, and this is highly probable, then Abdul Hamed el Atraqchi will send me

121

the money with which to pay the horse traders, and I shall have to bear nothing of the loss. And he thought: I am now truly a great merchant, for whereas before I used to buy cloth from the Baghdad merchants for fifty gold liras and I paid them cash, it took me a month to sell it and my profit was only seven gold liras. Now I am going to buy horses worth twenty thousand liras on credit, and if I make a profit it will be an enormous profit, yet if there is a loss it will be borne by the worthy Abdul Hamed el Atraqchi. So Abdul Rashid Mejid consented to the words of Kadhim.

Then Abdul Rashid Mejid sent his shop boy to the bazaar to tell the dealers that he wanted to buy horses. And the great horse dealers started to bring horses and mares to the shop of Abdul Rashid Mejid, and Kadhim hid himself in the shop, and when he gave a signal Abdul Rashid purchased the horse, and when no signal was given the horse was led away unpurchased. Kadhim knew most of the horses by sight, for the dealers were from the Fetla tribes, though some also were from Es Shammar and Ed Dulaim. And on Kadhim's instructions Abdul Rashid sent a message asking for three hundred men of the Fetla to look after the horses and act as grooms at a salary of one gold lira for every man for a month.

And all that day Abdul Rashid bought horses and the merchants of the bazaar thought him mad. And the horse dealers talked amongst themselves and said: Has Abdul Rashid enough money to pay for all these horses? And they said: He has been a merchant here for twenty-five years and he has never cheated anyone out of as much as a centimetre of cloth. He has always given credit to the men of the tribes and he has always conducted himself as an honourable man. But the more cautious amongst them said: Let us put two men to watch Abdul Rashid night and day, and should he try to leave Hilla before he settles for the horses, on that day let him meet the Angel of Death. And the others agreed and said: Let us adopt this course.

When two thousand horses and mares had been purchased Abdul Rashid Mejid ceased from the buying of horses. And Kadhim told him to order the grooms to bring food for their journey to Basra and grain for the horses. And these charges were written on the credit of Abdul Rashid Mejid. Then, in accordance with the instructions of Kadhim, Abdul Rashid told them to take the horses and start on the road for Basra at dawn on the next day and he told them that he who was in charge of the caravan would meet them on the road.

When the purchasing of the horses and the arrangements for the food and supplies were concluded Kadhim and Abdul Rashid Mejid sat in the shop and drank tea. And the heart of Abdul Rashid Mejid was full of wonder and he thought: At the rising of the sun this morning I did not owe a single copper coin to any man and now I owe twenty-two thousand four hundred and twelve gold liras and I am engaged in the great affairs of commerce. And as for Kadhim, he was thinking of Salma as he had seen her bathing in the river and he was thinking of the butterfly, and he said: O brother, how greatly am I enjoying our partnership and our co-operation. How I wish that I had a daughter that I might give her to you in marriage that we might be tied by a closer tie than that of trade, and how I wish that you had a daughter that I might marry her, for I am in need of a wife.

Abdul Rashid Mejid said: I have indeed a daughter of an age for marriage, and I was in fact about to give her to

123

one of our minor local merchants, in fact to this Abbas
Ali el Qassab whom you mentioned, the fellow who dyes
his beard and whose nose drips like the palm fronds
during rain. But if you desire her, let her be given to you
in marriage, that our partnership may be sealed.

And Kadhim replied: Let it be as you say, but first let
me go to Basra and sell the horses and conclude our
business, for I depart tomorrow at dawn and the marriage
will take a long time. Every day we delay lessens our
profit, for we have to feed the horses and pay the grooms.
But Abdul Rashid desired the marriage greatly, for he
thought: Perhaps when this great merchant gets back to
Basra he will change his mind, and it would be wise to tie
him to me by a closer tie than that of business, since,
should he forget or fail to send me the twenty-two
thousand four hundred and twelve gold liras, these horse
dealers will tear me limb from limb. But if I marry my
little darling Salma to him, then she can go with him and
remind him and see he sends the money.

So he said: A formal wedding indeed takes time, but
the ulema are my friends, and formalities break down
between friends and must be discarded when the needs of
business press and I think that I could arrange for you to
marry her this very night. The only difficulty that I can
foresee is that the girl may become hysterical, for she is
full of the foolishness of youth, but I will tell her that at
least your nose does not drip as do the palm fronds in rain.
And Kadhim agreed to the words of Abdul Rashid, and
he said: Let then the marriage be tonight and as for feasts
and formalities, let there be none, and as for the girl, tell
her that my nose does not drip and that I am a lover of
art and of beautiful things, such as butterflies. For Kadhim
knew that the mother of Salma had never told Abdul

Rashid about the butterfly, for he would have called it a useless expense.

Then Abdul Rashid Mejid hurried home to tell his wife and his daughter the great news, and he sent his shop boy to make the arrangements for the wedding. And he said to his daughter Salma: O little darling, how good is your luck. I am marrying you tonight to a great merchant of Basra. His name is Abdul Hamed el Atraqchi and he is so rich that twenty thousand gold liras is to him a mere nothing. But Salma cast herself on the ground and she sobbed great sobs, for she thought: Kadhim will kill Abbas Ali el Qassab, but he does not know of this new threat and I cannot see him before tonight.

Abdul Rashid Mejid said: Do not weep, my little daughter, for he is a handsome man and his nose is as dry as the desert at the end of summer and he tells me that he is a lover of beautiful things such as butterflies. And Salma's eyes dried when she heard her father's words, for she thought: Only my mother and Kadhim and no other person in the whole world knows about that butterfly. This is a signal from him. And her father thought: How my little daughter does hate dripping noses. Why, her face has become full of joy and her eyes are like the desert flowers in spring. And the heart of Abdul Rashid was glad that his daughter was happy, for he loved his daughter greatly.

So that night Kadhim went to the house of Abdul Rashid Mejid and he took the girl Salma in marriage, and when he took her from her father's house he took her to a black tent of the Arabs, for he had no other residence. And in the morning Kadhim and Salma rode out upon the Basra road, and they each rode one of the horses which had been purchased, though Salma had never even ridden a horse before, for she was a town girl, and it is said of the Arab girls of the towns that they cannot tell the difference between a horse and a water buffalo.

And on the road they met the men of the Fetla who were acting as grooms and they met the two thousand horses. And Kadhim was still wearing his rich clothes, but he had removed his beard, and he rode up to them and said: Do you know my face? And they replied: Are you not Kadhim the son of Qais? From whence are these clothes? And Kadhim replied: Know you that I am now rich and these horses are my horses, and I have married a girl. They said: Kadhim, are you then married and we did not eat as much as the leg of a sparrow at the feast? And Kadhim replied: You shall be my guests when we reach Basra, and when we get these horses safely there, then I shall reward you. But some of them said: How many of these horses will reach Basra? We shall be surprised if one hair from a mare's ear reaches there in safety. For how many tribes lie in our road and do not they all love horses? And Kadhim said: Put these thoughts from you, for every horse and every mare shall arrive safely. And they said: But how can this thing be?

Then Kadhim called out by name twenty men whom he knew and who were clever, and he ordered them and said: You shall ride ahead and go to every sheikh of every tribe on our road and you shall greet them and say: Know you that a sickness has come upon our horses and of them fifty are dying every day, but we are sending two thousand of them to the sea, in the hope that bathing them in the salt water may improve their condition and cure the sickness, though we have little hope that half of them will reach the sea alive. And we warn you, noble sheikhs, to keep your animals far from the Basra road,

126

that they may not catch the sickness, and we for our part
will keep our horses away from your animals, nor will we
approach any well at which you are watering. And the
men rode out to execute Kadhim's order.

The messengers rode out and they rode to the guest
tents and guest houses of all the sheikhs on the road to
Basra and they delivered Kadhim's message, and many of
the sheikhs were angry and said: We will not let you
enter our territory, for you may give us the sickness. But
the messengers said: If you oppose us then you must fight
us on horses, since we are mounted, and perhaps your
horses will catch the sickness from our horses. So the
sheikhs ordered their tribes to keep far from the horses of
the Fetla, and this order was obeyed.

Then Kadhim made the journey to Basra by forced
marches and he camped only on seven nights and he
camped away from people and from wells, and he spent
the nights in a black tent with Salma and he taught her
the customs of the tribes.

On the morning of the eighth day they saw Basra in
front of them, and they had not lost a single horse, and
Kadhim brought his caravan of horses up to the walls of
the city, and made ready to enter. But a Turkish officer
came out and commanded them: Go far from here, for
we hear there is a sickness amongst your horses. But
Kadhim took the officer and showed the horses to him,
and the officer saw that they were all fit and well. Then
Kadhim made the officer a present of ten horses and he
permitted them to enter the city.

In Basra the price of horses was three times the price in
Hilla, and though Kadhim gave each man of the Fetla one
horse to sell for his personal profit, he finished the sale of
the horses with the sum of twenty-two thousand four

hundred and twelve gold liras in one hand and a profit of twenty-eight thousand gold liras on the other hand. And he split the profit of twenty-eight thousand gold liras and took fourteen thousand gold liras for himself and he added the other fourteen thousand gold liras to the sum he owed Abdul Rashid Mejid. Then from his own share he bought a house at Basra for Salma, and he bought her copper cooking-pots and a gold bangle and two anklets of silver, and he engaged for her servants that she might not have to draw water from the river. And Kadhim tarried awhile at Basra, spending the time in the making of love and its enjoyment.

And in Hilla Abdul Rashid Mejid sat in his shop and there was fear in his heart, for he thought: When will my partner come or send the money. For he saw that the tribesmen sent by the horse dealers were watching him, and where he went there they followed. And one day there came to Hilla a wealthy merchant from Basra and Abdul Rashid went to him and asked: Is there news of the Basra merchant, Abdul Hamed el Atraqchi? Is he in good health? And the merchant replied: His name is not known to me. Then Abdul Rashid's heart stopped through fear, and he said: Is he not the wealthy merchant at the Khan of the Indian? And the merchant replied: My shop is in the Khan of the Indian, and I do not recognise his name. Then Abdul Rashid became as one mad, and he sat in his shop and would do no business and he wrung his hands as the washerman wrings clothes, and the horse dealers waited for their money.

One day Kadhim said to his wife Salma: I must go now to Hilla, and pay the money that I owe to your father. And Kadhim went to a banker of Basra and he gave him the forty thousand four hundred and twelve gold liras belonging to Abdul Rashid Mejid; and he took from him a draft on Baghdad for that amount. Then he mounted his horse and rode to Hilla. And before he entered the town he put on the beard of sheep's wool and became as Abdul Hamed el Atraqchi, the wealthy merchant, and he rode up to the shop of Abdul Rashid Mejid.

Now, when Abdul Rashid Mejid saw him his fury knew no bounds, and he ran out of the shop cursing Abdul Hamed and using to him names which politeness forbids me to mention. And Abdul Rashid tried to catch and lay hold of Abdul Hamed the merchant, but he was an old man and he could not catch him, and Kadhim rode out of the town thinking: This was a fine reception from my father-in-law. I will teach him a lesson.

Then Kadhim took off his beard and his headcloth and his shoes and his coat and rich clothes and he entered the town on foot wearing only a ragged thob, and he went up to the shop of Abdul Rashid and said: Take your gold liras and give me back my pledge. Abdul Rashid remembered the youth who had taken the gold liras and the cloth against the pledge of a hair of his moustache, so he took the money and he opened the box of pledges and he searched amongst the riding canes and headcloths and rings but he could not find the hair of Kadhim's moustache. It was but a small one, and it had got caught in some headcloth and whisked out of the box. And so he said to Kadhim: The pledge is lost, but it was of no value. Then Kadhim said: Is then a hair of my moustache a thing of no value? You give me that hair or I want your life, for that hair contains my honour. And Kadhim cursed Abdul Rashid, and the curses which he used (may they be far from you) were the curses with which Abdul Rashid had cursed Abdul Hamed el Atraqchi.

And after Kadhim was satisfied with cursing Abdul Rashid he drew out the draft for forty thousand four hundred and twelve gold liras and he gave it to Abdul Rashid and said: Know you that I am your son-in-law and Abdul Hamed el Atraqchi was but a dream. And Abdul Rashid looked at the draft and he saw that it was good and his heart was full of joy.

Then Kadhim returned to Basra and on the road it rained, and the rains were the first cold rains of winter, and Kadhim's clothes became wet and he caught cold, so that when he entered his house in Basra and greeted his wife Salma his nose was dripping even as the palm fronds drip in the rain, and Salma saw and she laughed much, nor did she weep at the dripping of Kadhim's nose.

THE STORY OF KHALID, THE

COPPERSMITH OF NASIRIYA

Let the name of Mohammed Hassan be written, that he is the teller of this story.

ONCE, in the days when the Turks ruled Iraq, there was a coppersmith of Basra, and Khalid was his name. He was born in Nasiriya, and lived there until the sixteenth year of his life. Then, when his father died, he took his mother and went to Basra and he worked as a coppersmith in the bazaar of Umm el Brum, that he might earn enough with which to live. Now, the amount he earned each month from the owner of the coppershop was only enough for food and rent and clothes for his mother and himself, nor could he save money enough to buy a shop of his own or to marry a wife. And Khalid and his mother lived in a poor house, and she did the cooking and all the work of the house was in her hands.

There came a day that the mother of Khalid fell sick and died and he was left alone in the house, nor was there anyone to do the cooking and the work of the house. As for Khalid, he had to go to work from the rising of the sun until its setting, so he could not go to the bazaar to buy vegetables and meat, nor could he cook his food. He therefore thought: Since I do not earn enough to keep a servant it is necessary that I marry a wife, and this course I would surely take if I had the money, since it is incumbent on a man to take to himself a wife. But since I have little money, let me seek out one who is less desired by men for some reason, that she may be cheap, and though she may not be perfect in all the requirements of a wife, she will at least buy the supplies from the market and cook them and clean the house.

Then Khalid sent for a wise woman who acted as a go-between for those about to marry, and he said to her: Know you that my income is small and my capital is none and I desire to marry a wife. Therefore seek out one whose father will not require of me more than one gold lira, and if she is lame or has only one eye, it matters not, but let her be able to cook. And the wise woman replied and said: I already know of such a one. Her father requires only a date stone. She is perfect in figure and in her face she has the beauty of the moon, she can recite poetry, and as for her cooking, verily it is said that there is a commotion in the heavens, for it is necessary to restrain the angels that they come not down to partake of it whenever she cooks a dish.

Khalid then said to the wise woman: If she be indeed as you say, then why the date stone? Perchance her name is dishonoured and such a one I do not want. But the woman said: If she be not a virgin, then return her to her father. Verily she is honourable, and as for the reason for the date stone, let it be known to you that this girl has the temper of a fiery steed, and her father has recently taken a wife of the same age as this girl, and she beats and torments the new wife of her father without mercy, nor is there peace in his house. Therefore he will give her to you in marriage and her name is Khalila. But she needs a firm hand on the reins. Khalid was happy that he should get a wife beautiful in face and figure, so he said to the wise woman: It shall be as you say. I shall marry this girl, and I shall control her, nor can her temper matter to me, for I am a man, and she is but a woman.

And so the arrangements were made and a day came on which Khalid sat in his house and his friends went and brought the girl Khalila to him and he took her in marriage. And Khalid's heart was filled with joy, for he found that the girl was beautiful of face and beautiful of figure and he spent the night in the delights and joy of matrimony, and he was happy and thought: I am only a poor

coppersmith, yet I have a bride fit for the Sultan himself.
And after a few days spent in married bliss Khalila woke
Khalid at the rising of the sun and she said to him: Rise
and go to your work, for the house is dirty and it needs
cleaning and attention. And Khalid rose and he went to
his work.

At the setting of the sun the coppersmiths in the bazaar
of Umm el Brum closed their shops and Khalid's master
permitted him to go and return to his home. And Khalid
entered his house and he stood and rubbed his eyes, for he
thought he was in a dream and that what he saw could
not be true. For his house was carpeted with the most
beautiful carpet made of silk, and it was truly worth not
less than one hundred gold liras, and on it stood chairs and
tables made of the finest woods, and on the tables were
dishes and vases of silver. And Khalid saw that his house
looked richer than that of the wealthiest merchant in
Basra, and he was amazed at what he saw.

And he said to his wife Khalila: From whence is this
wealth? She replied and said: Did you think that I was
going to live in a mud hut with no carpet, and with
chairs and tables of white deal, and with dishes of earthenware? I am of gentle birth and I need delicate and beautiful
things. Therefore have I pledged your credit and brought
these few poor things we need, and even this was difficult,
for the merchants did not seem to think much of your
ability to pay. And Khalid became angry and he said:
Woman, what have you done? Know you it will take
me fifty years to pay for this merchandise? She replied:
Am I then to live in squalor? Are you not a man that
you cannot pay for the needs of the house?

Then Khalid's fury grew, and it was in his thoughts
that he should beat his wife, and he picked up a stick and

134

got in a few blows on her, but when he put out his hand to hold her in one place that he might beat her the better, she bit his wrist to the bone, and it became apparent to Khalid that his wife had indeed the temper of a fiery steed.

The night passed in fighting and quarrelling and in the morning Khalid's face was covered with scratches from the finger-nails of his wife, and as for Khalila, her back was bleeding and her eyes were yellow from blows. And at the rising of the sun Khalila stayed in her bed, and she refused to make the breakfast for Khalid, and he went to his work hungry and empty, without even a sip of tea.

Khalid sat in the shop of the coppersmith and he fashioned vessels of copper and brass according to the orders of his master, but his heart was full of sadness and grief, and he thought: It was better that I had not married this girl, for now I am indebted to the extent of several hundred gold liras, whereas before I did not owe a single copper coin. And as for my food, she will not prepare it, for she is a fine lady. And at the setting of the sun Khalid sought out a wise woman who lived in the market and he said to her: My state is thus and thus. How can I tame my wife and make her obedient to me?

The woman thought much and she questioned Khalid concerning the nights of bliss, for she was an expert in these matters, and she said: When you go to your house you shall refrain from your wife and remain far from her, and this shall be for many days. Then shall you arrange to marry another wife, but I promise you that she will come to her senses and be obedient to you before this happens.

Khalid returned to his house and he entered, but he did not greet his wife. Instead he went to the carpet and stroked it with his hand and he said: O lovely carpet, how beautiful is your silken pile, how gay your colours. Verily, beauty is reserved to carpets only, nor do women have any share of it, for women are all alike. They have hair as black as a spider's legs, a pair of eyes similar to the eyes of a dog, mouths like monkeys' mouths, breasts like the udders of a water buffalo, and their skin is the colour of mud. How, then, can a man love a woman? But you, dear carpet, are of many gay colours, you have the colour of red roses, the blue of the morning sky, the green of young grass, and the yellow sheen of gold. What is more, you have the precious gift of silence, nor do you speak in shrill tones as do the cats when they fight in the moonlight. And that night and on the next night and on every night Khalid rolled up the carpet and took it with him to bed, nor did he speak to his wife. And as for Khalila, she thought: Unhappy is my lot, for I am married to a madman.

Now, let it be known to you that in those days the Turkish Governor of Basra kept a spy at Baghdad, that he might receive information and warning that he be not surprised by his superiors, for truly the revenue of Basra was great, and the Governor took more than three-quarters of it for himself and for the expenses of his house, and the remainder he sent to Baghdad, saying: Basra is but a poor city.

One day the Governor received a letter from his spy at Baghdad, and the letter read as follows:

O honoured and respected Governor, Let it be known to you that through the exercise of my secret trade I have discovered that a spy has been sent to Basra, and he has been ordered to report on your administration, and on the several revenues of the City. And as for his name, I know it not, and even if I knew it, then it would be of no value, for he would change it. But he is said to be such a man as would work as a smith or artisan, and I enjoin Your Honour to be on your guard against this dangerous man.

The Governor read the letter and his face turned as pale as milk, and he sent for his agents and spies, of whom he had many in the City of Basra, that they might inform him which of the merchants hid and concealed their wealth from him. And he said: Go to the bazaars and to the markets and make full enquiries concerning the smiths and artisans in this City, and inform me of one who is not a native of this place, and who is different from what he appears to be.

The spies and agents went off to execute the orders of their master the Governor, and for a whole week they made discreet enquiries in the bazaars and coffee-houses and they came back and reported to their master and they said: We have enquired diligently concerning every smith and every artisan of this City, and we have found one who says he comes from Nasiriya, and his name is Khalid. But these facts may be false, and he is certainly other than what he appears to be. For though he is only a poor coppersmith earning less than one gold lira a month, yet his house is furnished in a richer fashion than is your palace, and his wife goes to the market and she buys silken carpets and silver vessels worth hundreds of gold liras without a thought to the price.

The Governor dismissed them from his presence, and he thought: Verily this is he, for no doubt he was given a bag of gold for his expenses, and he has misappropriated the money for his own ends. And the Governor sent for his secretary, and this man enjoyed the fullest confidence of his master, and he said to his faithful secretary: The situation is thus and thus. Let us kill this dangerous man.

But the secretary thought for a long time, and then he

spoke after this fashion: To kill him would be folly, for another might come in his place. The Government has many hands and many eyes. Let us rather do another thing, let us incline this man to our side, for it is said that the heart of a man may be turned either by women or by gold. And the Governor agreed with his secretary and approved his words.

So the next day the secretary of the Governor went to the market of the coppersmiths and he went to the shop in which Khalid worked. And the master of the shop was pleased at his distinguished visitor, and he ordered a glass of tea from the coffee-house. But the secretary did not speak to the master of the shop. He turned to Khalid, and he examined the copper bowl he was making, and he said: This is indeed the best workman in Basra. And the master of the shop thought: Has the Governor's secretary been attracted by the eyes of our Khalid, for that bowl is no better and no worse than hundreds of others in this bazaar?

Then the secretary spoke and said: Know you that my master, the Governor, is always careful of the welfare of the people of Basra, and he is a lover of artistic and beautiful things, and he has heard that some of the copper vessels in the houses of the people of Basra are lacking in beauty and in skilful workmanship. Therefore has he commanded me that I find the most skilful coppersmith in Basra, that he may be appointed Inspector of Coppersmiths, and after due enquiry I find that you are indeed the best. I therefore appoint you Inspector of Coppersmiths at a salary of one hundred gold liras per month, and your duty shall be to inspect and license the coppersmiths of Basra, and you may charge them such fees as you deem suitable.

Khalid heard the words of the secretary, and his heart

was filled with a great joy, and as for the master of the shop, he thought: I knew that Khalid was a handsome young man, but I never thought that he would come to this, for it must be his beauty that the secretary admires, for as for his skill, it is not great.

Khalid thanked the secretary and he got up and left the coppersmith's shop, nor did he continue to work. And he went to his house to tell his wife to pack the furniture that they might move from the mud house to a house of marble and fine stones. And Khalid entered his house and he said to his wife: Pack the carpet and furniture that we may move to a palace fit for our high estate.

Khalila heard the words of her husband and her heart was filled with grief, and she thought: Truly I have driven this poor man mad, for he is only a poor coppersmith unable to find the money for even this house. Yet he talks of moving to a palace. How unlucky is my lot, for even if he divorces me, who will marry a divorced woman? And it appears I shall spend my life married to a madman, and never again shall I taste of the joys of marriage.

So Khalila cast herself at her husband's feet, and her body vibrated with sobs, and she said: O my husband, only be as you were on the night of our wedding, and you may take a stick and beat me as much as your heart desires, for I merit a beating. And Khalid thought: She indeed merits a beating, and if I do this to her she will be obedient in future. So he took a stick and beat his wife until the blood came, nor did she fight or resist him.

Then Khalid took his wife and he moved to a fine house and he spent many years in the enjoyment of love and in drawing the emoluments of his high office. And Khalila returned his love exceedingly and she obeyed him in everything, and as for the Governor of Basra, he was happy for he thought that he had inclined the heart of the Government spy towards him. And as for the real spy, he was never heard of, for he was set on and killed by the Maadan on his way to Basra, and they took from his body his bag of gold, nor did the Government send another spy in his place.

THE STORY OF THE SON OF

THE PILGRIM

Verily man cannot die before his appointed time, nor can he live after it for even as long as it takes a stone to drop from the hand to the ground.

ONCE in ancient times there was or there was not a great landowner, master of vast estates, to whom the sheikhs of the Arabs and of the bedouin paid tribute and in God only is there belief.

The name of the landowner was Hassan, and he had a young wife beautiful as a moon, and a faithful slave who had been with him since boyhood and whose name was Ahmed, and Ahmed was devoted to his master and obeyed him in everything.

There came a year in which the Sultan sent a command to the landowner Hassan, and he appointed him Prince of the caravan which was setting out on the Pilgrimage. The wife of Hassan was at that very time with child, and Hassan loved her greatly, nor did he like to leave her. So he ordered that a seat and canopy should be prepared for her on a camel, and he said: It is fitting that my son be born on the Pilgrimage.

The Pilgrimage set out and its destination was Mecca, and it marched according to the orders of the Prince of the Caravan, and with him went his wife and Ahmed his faithful slave. And the caravan reached the Valley of Tos and halted there for the night. Now, with the caravan were many Indian pilgrims, and amongst them was the sickness of cholera, and in the Valley of Tos the sickness spread to many men and many women in the caravan, and they rolled on the ground in the agony of death.

And on that very night the child in the wife of Hassan reached his appointed hour for entering the world, and Hassan said to his faithful slave: Summon the midwife and the wet nurses. For he had arranged for them to be with the caravan. But the slave Ahmed answered and said: Master, they are dead of the sickness. Then Hassan and the slave Ahmed attended themselves to the wife of Hassan

142

and they brought forth from her a fine boy and he lived, but as for Hassan's wife, she died in the pangs and labour of childbirth. Then Hassan asked the slave Ahmed to enquire if there was any woman in the caravan who could nurse the boy, but Ahmed returned and said: Master, we of this caravan are now only of one sex, for those women who were amongst us are dead, and even the camels are not in milk.

Hassan's heart was full of grief and he thought: My beloved wife is dead and now my son will die, and he ordered Ahmed: Dig a tomb and place in it my wife and my son. Ahmed said: Master, will you, then, bury a living boy? Hassan answered: Is there, then, milk in your breast that you will nurse him? Rather should we leave him to the will of God. So the slave Ahmed dug a tomb and he placed in it the woman and the boy, and the boy still lived.

In the morning after they had buried those who had died of the sickness the caravan marched on, and they came to the valley of Faratos, where they camped for the night. The sickness had not departed from them, and the night was filled with the screams of the dying. And the Prince of the Caravan fell sick and he died on that very night.

And in the morning the slave Ahmed looked around him and he saw that he was the only one of that company to rise from the ground to say the morning prayer, and as for the rest of them they were all in the stillness of death. The slave Ahmed collected the camels and the bags of money and supplies, and he tied the body of his master to a camel, for he thought: It is fitting that the Prince of the Caravan should complete the Pilgrimage.

The slave Ahmed loaded the camels and set out on the road to Mecca, and he arrived there after a journey free from further misfortunes. At Mecca he remained for many months, and he sold the camels and the property of his master, for there were too many camels for one man to look after and he collected the sums of money and put them with the gold he had taken from the caravan, and he kept careful account of all these sums.

Then he thought and pondered after this fashion: What shall I do with all this money, for my master is dead, his wife is dead, and his son is dead, and his only heir is his brother? And although it is true that his brother will take my master's great estates and land, and this I cannot prevent, for I am only a poor slave, yet he should not have this gold as well, for verily there was hatred between these two brothers. And he decided thus: I will take this gold and return to our land, and if, please God, I arrive in safety, I will give the money to the mosques and to religious charities, that the name of my master may be remembered with honour.

The slave Ahmed waited for the rains, that the wells might be full and his journey easy, then he set out alone with a few camels, and his destination was Iraq. And in the course of his journey he came to the valley of Tos, and it was in his thoughts to attend the tomb of his mistress, and to repair it from the ravages of time. So when he had unloaded the camels and prepared his camp he walked over to the tomb of his mistress.

Ahmed looked at the tomb of his mistress and he saw that there was a hole in the roof, and he looked down through the hole and he was filled with amazement and surprise, for he saw in the tomb a living boy. Then Ahmed dragged aside the stones and opened the tomb, and he saw that the boy was about one year of age, and that the body of his mistress was decayed and withered away, except for one breast, which was alive and full. Ahmed took the child in his arms and in that very instant the remaining breast withered and decayed and faded away.

Ahmed took the child and walked over to his camels, and amongst the camels was a she camel in milk, and he took a vessel and filled it with milk and he gave it to the child and he drank.

The next day Ahmed continued his journey and he thought: I will go to Hail and there halt for some years, until my young master is grown. If we go now to Iraq the boy's uncle may do some evil thing, for he will by now have occupied the estates, and I am but a poor slave, and I will not be able to get my young master his rights. Fortunately we have plenty of gold and I can educate him in a manner fitting to his estate. Then, when he is a grown man, he can claim his land.

So Ahmed took the boy and he journeyed to Hail, and when he arrived there he bought a house and hired a nurse for the child, and when some years had passed he hired for him a teacher, and he educated him also in the use of the sword and the spear in horsemanship and in the arts of war.

There came a day that the boy was grown to sixteen years of age, and he was the handsomest of all the boys in Hail, and his beauty was unsurpassed, and as for his skill with the sword, there was none in Hail to equal him. And Ahmed came to him and said: Master, know you that I am but your slave and not your guardian as you had thought. And Ahmed related to his young master Rejab those facts and those events with which you, my listeners, are acquainted, and Rejab was amazed at what he heard.

Then Rejab ordered his slave Ahmed to prepare camels for their journey to Iraq, and Ahmed sold the house and prepared for the journey, and there was with him a large bag of gold, for he had been careful of his master's wealth.

After many days on the road Rejab and his slave Ahmed came to Iraq, and to the estates of his father, which were near to Samawa. And they inquired in the villages and from the people concerning the situation and they replied: Hamed the brother of Hassan has inherited the estates and he has been in occupation of them for the last sixteen years. And verily he is a tyrant, for he takes from the poor even their bread. And Rejab and his slave Ahmed kept their identity a secret, and to those who asked of Ahmed concerning his master he replied: He is a young prince of the Shammar from Hail, and since he has no work or occupation he travels for his amusement. Rejab and Ahmed camped in a black tent of the Arabs near to Samawa, and they had only their animals for company.

One dark night before the rising of the moon Rejab and Ahmed were asleep in the tent and Ahmed awoke and heard a noise. So he took his sword and dashed out, thinking: Thieves are at the camels. He ran to the animals and found near them an old bent man with a long white beard, and the old man asked of him food and water. So Ahmed took the old man to the tent and he woke his young master, and Rejab ordered that the old man be given food and water, and he ate until he was satisfied. Then the old man thanked Rejab, and he said: I will sell you two sayings for a coin of Damascus. Ahmed searched in the bag of money until he found a coin of Damascus and he gave it to the old man. Then the old man spoke after this fashion: As for the first saying, Thou shalt beware of the one-eyed man, and as for the second saying, Thou shalt not sleep on the nights of the new moon. And the old man took his staff and rose and hobbled away.

In the morning Rejab said to Ahmed his slave: We are

146

camped here without benefit, for no plan presents itself by which I may regain my estates, and verily if I say to the people, I am the son of Hassan and I lived for a year in my mother's tomb, no man will believe me. Rather should I go to my uncle's guest-house and see what manner of man he be, and if he be not evil, I should say, I am your nephew. But the slave Ahmed said: Verily he is evil. And Rejab replied: How can this be, for he is of my own blood?

So Rejab and his slave rode to the guest-house of Hamed and Rejab entered and saluted the assembly. He saw that there was a great coming and going of people. So when the slave brought him coffee he asked: What is this great throng? And the slave replied: Know you that tonight the daughter of our master will be given in marriage, and people have come in from the whole district to be at the feast. And Rejab asked the slave: Is she beautiful? And the slave answered: Verily when my mistress comes out at night, then the moon hides its face, for it is jealous of her beauty. Rejab thought: It is my right as her cousin to marry this girl. I should see my uncle and declare myself.

Rejab sat for half an hour in the guest-house. Then there was a commotion and the people rose, for the land-owner Hamed entered to partake of his morning coffee, and Rejab saw the face of his uncle. And he was amazed, for Hamed had only one eye. And Rejab turned to his neighbour in the assembly and he said: I never knew our host was one-eyed. The man replied: It was only a month ago that it happened. Our master was stroking and petting his hawks, and the falconer had put a new bird with them and he knew it not, and this hawk took out his eye as cleanly as it would take out the eye of a hare. And Rejab thought: The saying of the old man was surely a warning

147

against my uncle. I must not reveal my identity to him.

So Rejab sat in the guest-house, and he was thinking: It is my right to marry this girl. How can I prevent the marriage? And Hamed looked around his guest-house and he saw a strange youth of great beauty seated there, and he asked: Who is he? They answered: He is one of the Shammar princes from Hail, and we do not know his name. Then Rejab rose and thanked his host and left the assembly, and he took his horse and rode off. But when he was in the cover of the palm trees he halted and turned to look at the house of Hamed, for he thought: I must carry off the girl this very day. He saw that the women's quarter was heavily guarded by slaves and eunuchs armed with swords, and all the doors to the courtyard were guarded, nor was it possible to gain entrance. But he saw also that the House of the Dawn was situated at a distance from the house, that its odours (may they be far from you) should not disturb the people of the house, and he cursed himself and thought: Had I come one day earlier I could have carried off the girl when she comes at dawn to visit the House of the Dawn, but now there is no time to wait another day. Then an idea came to him, and he took his horse and rode at a canter to Samawa.

In the bazaar of Samawa, Rejab bought first a woman's dress, and he wrapped it up and concealed it in his cloak. Then he went to the pharmacist and he bought three Roman pills. Now, let it be known to you that in these days we have many and complicated medicines, but then we had only simple remedies, and the Roman pill served both for a man and for his animals, for verily it was said, One for a man, two for a horse, three for a camel. And he took the three Roman pills and he went to the shop of the sweet maker and he bought from him a tray of the

148

finest sweets, and he cut open the largest and the best
sweet and placed inside it the three Roman pills, saying to
the sweetmaker: My she-camel will not take pills, therefore I have to conceal them in sweets.

Rejab mounted his horse and rode back to his tent, and
there he ordered his slave Ahmed to load the animals, and
to take them to a mound which was eight hours' march
out into the desert on a little used route. Then he mounted
a fresh horse, and taking the woman's clothes and the
sweets under his cloak, he rode out to the house of Hamed.
But when he was near to the house he took his horse and
tethered it in the concealment of the palm trees near to the
House of the Dawn. Then he put on the woman's clothes
and hid his own clothes near his horse, and he put the tray
of sweets on his shoulder and walked towards the house,
crying in a girl's voice: Buy my sweets and buy luck. And
his veil he let fall after the manner of gypsies, for his
moustache was not grown, and he was beautiful to behold,
and the slaves and sentries who saw him thought: What
a pretty gypsy girl is this. Perchance we can have some
fun with her this night. And they let Rejab enter the
courtyard of the harem.

Then the women servants came crowding around
Rejab and they wanted to buy sweets, but he gave them
not, saying: First I must sell the largest sweet for a piece
of silver to her who is about to marry, for it will bring her
luck and a fine boy child. And the women cried: Take the
gypsy girl to our mistress, that she may be cheered up, for
verily she is weeping now, for she likes not this marriage.

They took Rejab and led him into the chamber in
which was seated the Lady Aliya, the daughter of Hamed,
and she was weeping in a manner to tear the heart. And
the maids and servants said to her: Mistress, buy a sweet

149

from the gypsy girl, that it may bring you luck and a fine boy child. And Rejab looked at the Lady Aliya and his heart was full of joy, for verily her eyes were like pearls, her mouth was like a rosebud, her breasts were revealed by the silken cloth of her dress, and lovely was their shape, and her body was as slim as that of a boy.

The Lady Aliya looked through her tears at the gypsy girl and she said: Give me, then, a sweet, though it cannot bring me happiness, for my grief is beyond help. And Rejab gave the Lady Aliya the largest sweet, and she ate it and said: On the outside it was sweet and delicious, but its centre was bitter. Why was this? And Rejab replied: Lady, this was a sweet of love, for know you that love is sweet, but it is not without bitterness, for love must end and all lovers will be parted if only finally by death. Therefore first a girl tastes the sweets of love, but afterwards she must taste its bitterness and grief.

And the Lady Aliya thought: How wise are the words of the gypsy girl. And she ordered that the girl be rewarded with a gold lira. And Rejab took the coin and he gave the remaining sweets to the servants, saying: Take these free, for your mistress has paid me handsomely, and I must go now and hurry to my tent and make many more sweets, for there will be a great demand for them this night. And Rejab left the chamber and left the courtyard, and the sentries and guards called out to him: O my pretty one, wilt thou return tonight? And Rejab winked at them and answered: Verily I shall be at your disposal this night. And he hurried away to the palm trees and to his horse.

The Lady Aliya sat in her chamber thinking: How pretty was that gypsy girl and how brazenly she looked at me with her eyes. It was almost as if she desired my body.

And how bitter was the centre of her sweet. For the Lady Aliya knew not that the sweet contained three Roman pills, the dose for a camel.

When Rejab reached his horse he stripped off the clothes of a girl and he put on his own clothes, and he strapped on his sword, and he stood by his horse, watching the House of the Dawn and thinking: It will not be long now. And after ten minutes he saw the Lady Aliya come out of the gate of the courtyard and her step was the step of one in haste, and she made towards the House of the Dawn. And when the Lady Aliya was near the House of the Dawn, but before she could enter it, Rejab rode down on her and seized her in his arms and pulled her across his horse, and he covered her mouth with his hand, nor could she utter a scream, and he turned his horse and galloped off in the direction of the desert. And with such dash and speed did he do this that the sentries saw nothing, for they were looking into the courtyard thinking: It is not fitting that we stare at the Lady Aliya while she walks towards the House of the Dawn.

When they had galloped some distance from the house of Hamed, Rejab released his hand from Aliya's mouth, and she looked at his face and she saw that he had the face of the pretty gypsy girl. And she thought: If my captor is indeed a man, and so it appears, then I am indeed in luck, for he is handsomer by far than that horrible old landowner to whom my father was going to marry me. But there was agony and pain in the stomach of Aliya, and she said: O noble stranger, let me down for a moment that I may ease myself. And Rejab replied: Wait until we are in the desert when we may see if we are pursued.

After they had entered the desert, and when there was a clear mile behind them to watch for pursuit, Rejab permitted the girl Aliya to get down and ease herself. And when she had done this she returned to his horse, nor did he have to catch her, and Rejab saw that she came with him freely. And she mounted the horse, and she said: Pardon the delay, but now let us ride on, that we may put many miles between my father and me. Then Rejab replied: As for the delay, it was necessary, for I gave you three Roman pills, the dose for a camel, that I might make sure. And Aliya answered: Verily you made sure that I would leave the house, for one of those Roman pills would have been enough. And Aliya laughed much at the stratagem of Rejab and she said: So this was the bitterness in the sweet of love. Then Rejab said: My darling, you who have tasted the bitterness at the beginning of our love will never have to taste it again, for there will be no end to our loving. And Aliya and Rejab discovered that they were of one heart.

Rejab took Aliya and he rode for eight hours into the desert until he came to the mound on the unfrequented track, and there they awaited the coming of the slave Ahmed with the animals. And after an hour's wait the slave arrived with the camels. They put up a black tent of the Arabs, and Aliya cooked food for them. And when they had eaten of the food, Rejab took Aliya into the black tent, and the slave Ahmed he ordered to stand on guard. And the girl Aliya trembled as Rejab took her into the tent, and Rejab said to her: Do not fear, for I am close to you, nor am I far, and I am he who has the right to marry you and the right to kill you. Then Aliya was astonished, and she said: But he who would have the right to marry me and the right to kill me would be my cousin, yet cousin have I none. And Rejab replied: I am indeed he. And he related the full story of his birth and his life in the tomb, and Aliya was astonished at what she heard.

Now, in the house of Hamed, after a period of time had passed, people began to ask: Where is the Lady Aliya? For the mother of the girl was calling, Aliya, Aliya, and yet there was no response. And Hamed the one-eyed became worried when he saw that his daughter was not in the house, and he questioned the sentries and said: Has the Lady Aliya gone out? And the sentries replied: Verily she passed out through this gate an hour ago, and she went towards the House of the Dawn. Yet we have not seen her return. And Hamed became anxious when he heard these words, for he thought: Perchance she has cut a vein or run away, for she wanted not this marriage. So he sent a slave girl to the House of the Dawn, saying: Report to me concerning your mistress.

The slave girl ran out to the House of the Dawn, and she found it empty, nor was there anyone there. Then Hamed ordered his slaves and guards to search the palm trees, and they went out and came back and reported: There is no one there, but we found these clothes belonging to a woman and this brass tray. Hamed examined the clothes, and the maids and the slave girls also came and examined them, and they said: These are not the clothes of our mistress. Rather, they are the clothes of the gypsy girl who sold the sweets. Then Hamed enquired of the guards at the gate, and one of them said: Truly I did not think of it at the time, for she was a girl and he was a boy, but the gypsy girl had verily the same face as the young Shammar prince who was here this morning, and they were as alike in the face as two hairs of a mare's tail.

Hamed was convinced by the words of the guard, and he said: My daughter has been taken by the Shammar prince. Does anyone know where his camp is? And one of the Arabs in the assembly said: I have heard that he is camped near the village of so and so. And Hamed ordered his steward: Ride to the camp of the Shammar prince, and take twenty men, and bring him here by force. And the steward took the men and rode off, but after two hours he returned and reported: His camp is struck and he is away into the desert with his animals. And the fury of Hamed knew no bounds and he said: What are these Shammar princes? Do they hang around the harem as do rats around the grain store? Then Hamed ordered his steward: Prepare every man we have got, that we may pursue him on the road to Hail.

And those that were there assembled said: Are you, then, a great sheikh, or are you only a landowner, that you go to war with the Shammar? For never will they give up this boy who is one of their princes. And are they not said to have ten thousand warriors? Hamed realised the truth of their words and he said: I will pursue them with every man I have, that I may catch them before the territory of the Shammar. But should they enter, then I need assistance. And Hamed wrote a letter to those sheikhs who were his neighbours and whose tribes rented his land, and he said: Give me help to avenge my honour, for my daughter is stolen. But the sheikhs replied and said: We sympathise and regret your situation, and touching on your honour, you will know how to defend it, and as for us, we will not meddle in the affair. For the sheikhs liked not Hamed, since he was a miser.

Then Hamed collected every slave and every man he had, but they numbered only three hundred, and he rode out along the road to Hail. And the people said: Is it thus that one goes to war with the Shammar?

From his camp in the desert Rejab sent his slave Ahmed daily to the towns and villages, that he might bring information, and so he heard of the reply of the sheikhs and of the departure of Hamed. And he thought: Now is my chance to regain my estates. So Rejab left the girl Aliya with the slave Ahmed and he rode to the encampment of the greatest sheikh whose tribe rented land from Hamed, and he entered the guest-house and saluted the assembly, and he told his name to the sheikh, saying: I am Rejab the son of Hassan who died on the Pilgrimage, and I have come to regain my estates. But the sheikh said: How can this thing be? For Hassan had no son, though his wife was pregnant when he left here, and they all died of cholera on the road, nor did a single one of that caravan survive. And Rejab told the story of his birth and of his life in the tomb to the sheikh, and that sheikh was amazed at what he heard.

Then the sheikh said: You will honour us by taking a meal? And Rejab accepted the hospitality of the sheikh. Then the sheikh went out of the guest-house, and he ordered the slaves to bring food, and Rejab sat in the guest-house and he waited the coming of the meal. And after a time the slaves brought in the meal, and Rejab was amazed at what he saw, for instead of a mound of rice on the great dish there was a mound of steaming hot earth, and on the mound of earth there was the skeleton of a sheep, nor was there any meat on its bones. And Rejab turned to the sheikh and he said: Is this not a strange meal that you set before me? The sheikh replied: You as a child drank milk from the breast of a dead woman. It should be to you as nothing to get nourishment from the skeleton of a sheep and from a mound of steaming hot earth. But I am curious to see you do it, and after the meal is finished I will order the slave to bring you coffee made of hot ink.

Rejab saw that the sheikh did not believe his story, and he thought: How can I convince him, for this story is indeed difficult to believe? And Rejab spoke and said: As for nourishment, there is nourishment in the skeleton. For do not the flies settle on it, and they go nowhere to amuse themselves? They only seek nourishment, and as for me, I cannot now die, even without nourishment, for would God have kept me alive for a year in my mother's tomb to have me die now in the sixteenth year of my life? Shoot at me an arrow if you so desire, for it cannot kill me, since my death is not yet ordained.

The sheikh ordered a slave to bring him his bow, and he took an arrow, and he stood at a distance of ten paces from Rejab in the great guest-room, and he drew the bow taut and aimed it at Rejab, and he said: I ask your pardon if I kill you, my guest, and if I do not kill you, I ask your pardon that I doubted your word. And Rejab said: Shoot the arrow and as for my pardon, it is granted. And the sheikh saw that Rejab did not flinch, and he released the bow, and the arrow went wide.

Then the sheikh bid Rejab be seated and he brought for him coffee, and he said: Verily you are your father's son, and I will assist you to get your rights, for this dog Hamed pleases me not. And the sheikh called his sirkals and he said: This boy is the rightful heir of Hassan. Call four hundred men and instal him in his father's house. And the sirkals assembled the tribesmen and they rode to the house of Hamed, nor did the guards left by Hamed oppose their entrance. And Rejab called the tenants and told them that Hamed was evicted and that he was the rightful heir.

Then Rejab wrote a letter to Hamed his uncle:

To His Honour the Brother, the Respected and Dear Uncle,—After the customary greetings it behoves me to inquire about your health, and I, dear uncle, am praying for your health and safety. And know you that I am the son of your brother Hassan, and in your absence I have occupied my father's house and lands, which you have cared for so well, and on your return I will greet you as my guest if you come in peace, and if you come in anger then I am ready. And know you that your daughter Aliya is my wife, and she spends her days in praying for Your Honour's health.

And Hamed received the letter when he was within seven marches of Hail, and when he read it his face turned black with fury, and he said: Who is this foundling up-start? And the messenger said: Verily he is your brother's son.

Then Hamed turned his men and returned to Iraq. And his slaves said: Thank God we are not to fight the Shammar with this army. And after several marches Hamed came to his former house, and he saw that it was surrounded by the black tents of the tribesmen. Hamed was outnumbered, but such was his fury that he led his men in a charge. Rejab stood in front of the tribesmen, and verily the force of Hamed went down before the tribesmen as does wheat in hail. Rejab disarmed his uncle, but allowed him his life, for he said: The brother of my father I cannot kill, and the father of my wife I cannot kill.

Then Rejab took his wife Aliya and he lived in the house of his father in prosperity and peace, and when the nights passed and dawn came in the East, then Rejab and Aliya would walk together to the House of the Dawn which stood at a distance from their house, nor would he let her go there alone.

THE STORY OF THE CLOAK

WHICH WAS THE FATHER OF
A CHILD

ONCE, in the days of Haroun er Rashid, Abu Nawas the friend and companion of the Commander of the Faithful was walking amongst the tents and reed huts of the poor people who lived on the outskirts of Baghdad, in search of amusement for his master. And as he was passing a tent he heard in it voices and they were raised in anger, and they were speaking in the slow tones of the people of the high desert, and Abu Nawas stopped to listen to their words.

And a man's voice was speaking and its tones were the tones of fury and it said: O daughter, you shall tell me the name of the man who is the father of this child, that I may kill him and I may kill you and our name may be again among the honourable. And a girl's voice answered and said: O my father, verily there was no man. Know you that one night last winter I had gone to fetch water, and the ground was frosty and the night had the coldness of death, and I was trembling with cold and the fear of the night air, when I saw on the ground a man's cloak, and I picked it up and wrapped it around me and I became warm. But, alas, from the smell of that cloak there came in my stomach a child.

Abu Nawas thought: Verily this is an affair in which my master will be interested, for does he not take an interest in everything touching the welfare of his subjects? So Abu Nawas entered the tent, and he found there an old man whose face was creased in fury, and a young girl beautiful of the face who was weeping in a manner to turn the heart, and in the hand of her father was a dagger.

Abu Nawas commanded the man to lay his dagger aside and he said: Know you that I am a high officer of the State, and to disobey my orders will lose you your head. There is much in this affair of interest to justice. Therefore tomorrow shall you go to the Qadhi, and you shall take with you your daughter, and you shall take the cloak, and also the man who is the owner of the cloak, that the Qadhi may discover how there came into your daughter's stomach a child, that justice may be done.

Then Abu Nawas returned to the Palace and he related to the Commander of the Faithful that which had taken place, and Haroun er Rashid was pleased and he ordered: Bring me a disguise, for tomorrow I myself will sit in the Qadhi's court. So the next day Haroun er Rashid and Abu Nawas went to the court of the Qadhi, and the girl and her father and the cloak and the owner of the cloak were also present there

And the father of the girl was abashed and silent in the presence of the Qadhi and the people of the court, for he was from the high desert. And the Qadhi asked him: Whom do you accuse? But the bedawi remained silent. Then Abu Nawas stepped forward and said: O Qadhi, let me speak for him, for he is without a tongue. And permission was allowed for him to speak.

Abu Nawas pointed a finger at the cloak, and he said: O Cloak, verily I accuse you of the rape of this innocent young girl. For did you not wrap your woollen folds even around her naked thighs and did not your lecherous male smell enter into her and cause to become in her stomach a child? And the Qadhi was amazed at the words of Abu Nawas, and he asked: Have you evidence to prove your accusation? And Abu Nawas said: Let the girl give evidence.

The girl walked forward and she said: O learned Qadhi, verily I am innocent of all evil and of all offence, nor have I ever been near to a man. But it happened that last winter I went in the night to draw water from the River Tigris,

M   161 and there was frost on the ground, and I was trembling from cold and fear of the night. And as I walked along I saw in front of me on the path the cloak of a man, so I picked it up and wrapped it around me and I became warm. But, alas, though I knew it not at the time, from the smell of that cloak there came in my stomach a child. And the Qadhi thought: This is a most strange case and I like it not. For who is that huge merchant with the beard sitting in the crowd? He is almost big enough to be our lord and master Haroun er Rashid himself. And so the Qadhi questioned the girl, thinking: I must conduct this case according to the best and most learned rules of law, that the Commander of the Faithful be pleased with me.

The learned Qadhi asked the girl: What is your name? The girl replied: I am named Khadija, nor have I any other name. And the Qadhi wrote the reply of the girl in his great book. Then the Qadhi said to her and he asked of her: The accuser has stated that this cloak wrapped itself around your naked thighs. Did this indeed happen? And the girl Khadija replied: Verily it was so, for I was wearing a dress and my own black abba, and over it I put on this cloak of a man. And first it tickled me around my neck, so I pulled my dress up over my head so that my neck might be protected from its tickling. And when I did this that devil of a cloak wrapped its folds even around my naked thighs and it commenced tickling me a hundredfold in that region, so that I started to laugh and power departed from my legs and I fell to the ground. And such was its insistent tickling that I parted my legs and it may well have been that at this time its smell entered me and caused in my stomach a child.

The Qadhi turned to the assembly, and he asked: Does anyone speak for the accused, for being but a cloak it has

162

no tongue? Yet none can be condemned unheard, for such is the wise order of our mighty master Haroun er Rashid, the noble, the blessed. And the bearded merchant who was indeed none other than the Commander of the Faithful in person, came forward and said: I will defend the cloak.

The bearded merchant raised his hand and he said in a noble and loud voice: Verily the cloak is innocent, for does not the girl say that it was the smell which caused in her stomach to come a child? And the smell is different from the cloak and it merely rides on it in the manner that a man rides on a horse. It frequently happens that a rider returns from the desert to his house and he enters unto his wife and he causes in her stomach to come a child. Yet never have I heard it said that the horse was the father of the child. And on one cloak may ride many smells, such as the smell of tobacco, the smell of scent, the smell of coffee and other smells, in the manner that one horse may have many riders. It is the smell which you must accuse and try, and the cloak you must acquit.

The learned Qadhi gave judgement and said: O Cloak, you are free from blame. You may continue to be a cloak and be such a cloak as you have always been before. And I hereby order to be brought before me the smell which despoiled this innocent girl.

And Abu Nawas said: O Qadhi, the smell is on the cloak and it must surely be before you, and if you doubt it come and sniff. And Abu Nawas turned to the cloak and he pointed his finger at it and he said: O evil smell, riding upon an innocent cloak, verily you entered this maiden and you caused in her stomach to come a child.

The Qadhi turned to the people there assembled and he asked: Does anyone speak for the smell? And again the large merchant with a beard came forward and said: I will defend it.

Haroun er Rashid, for indeed it was he, raised his right hand and said: Verily the smell was innocent, for how can a smell know guilt? Do you accuse the arrow or do you accuse the man who shot it. O Qadhi, you must acquit the smell and accuse the owner of the smell. Then the Qadhi spoke and he gave judgement and said: O smell, you are found to be without guilt. Continue then to be a smell and smell as you have always smelled before.

Then the Qadhi ordered to be brought before him the owner of the smell, and they led a youth in the sixteenth year of his life in front of the Qadhi, and they said: This boy owns the cloak, therefore he must own the smell which goes with that cloak. And the Qadhi asked the boy: What is your name? The boy replied: Verily it is Karaim. Then the Qadhi said to the boy: Know you that you are accused of owning an active and dangerous smell, and, as you have failed to keep this smell under control you have caused in the stomach of this girl to exist a child. And the boy answered and said: Verily I am innocent of all wrong.

Then the Qadhi said to the boy: On the night that this girl found your cloak on the ground and she put it on to keep herself warm, where were you and why were you not controlling your smell? And the boy replied: On that bitterly cold night on which the girl put on my cloak to keep herself warm, verily I was inside the cloak and no-where else, for where else should a man be on a cold night but inside his cloak?

So the Qadhi called the girl and he said: Verily your evidence was incomplete and lacking accuracy, for why did you not say that when you found the cloak on the ground that bitterly cold night and you put it on to keep

164

yourself warm, that there was a boy in the cloak?

And the girl Khadija replied and said: Verily I had forgotten, for many months have passed since that night, and it is easy to forget what things contain. How often, O learned Qadhi, do you have to feel in your pockets to see if you have with you your key and your rosary and your money, when you took them from your house only a few minutes earlier? How much easier then, is it for me to have forgotten what that cloak contained after so many months.

The Qadhi then demanded of the boy Karaim: What is your reply to the accusation? Karaim raised his hand and answered: I am innocent, for I did but allow the girl to come and shelter in my cloak on that bitterly cold night. And do you, O Qadhi, blame the sheep when they huddle together in the frosty wind? For do not even the sheep know that two bodies are warmer than one, and are we, the sons of Adam, to be inferior to the sheep in this respect?

Then the Qadhi gave judgement and said: The boy is innocent and the girl is innocent of all wrong, nor shall the father of the girl have the right to kill them. But I do command and order that this boy and this girl be married this very day, that when the cold winds of winter blow he may cover her with his cloak and that they may huddle together to gain warmth.

THE STORY OF THE TWO

DANCERS

Let it be written that the story was related by Hamed, while we were awaiting the coming of the wild duck.

ONCE in Basra there was a dancing boy and a dancing girl and they were brother and sister. They were Circassians of great beauty, and they were slaves of a Turk who kept a dancing hall. So beautiful was their dancing that the great and noble Pashas and even the Wali of Basra himself would pay bags of gold to watch their dancing. And the boy, whose name was Nasirulla, and the girl, whose name was Salma, were displeased at their situation, for whatever gold they earned, the Turk took it, and it appeared to them that they would remain forever slaves.

One day the boy Nasirulla said to his sister: Know you that a time will come when our beauty will fade, and then these mighty Pashas will no longer want to gaze at our dancing. Then will our Turkish master sell us to do manual work on the roads and fields, and they will work us so hard that we shall die in a few years in agony and misery. But as for our master, he will be rich from all this gold which he takes from us, and he will buy a house and live in it with his mistresses while we are starving, and this state of affairs is neither right nor is it just. The girl Salma replied: Indeed, you speak the truth, but how are we to escape from this Turk? For in the daytime he is watchful, and at night does he not chain us by the neck with an iron chain? And Nasirulla replied: We must kill this man. Salma turned pale and she said: Do you not know the penalties for slaves who kill their masters? And how will this benefit us, since they will find him dead and then they will commence to flog us? Anyway, how can you kill him, since you are only a weak boy?

Then Nasirulla said to her: Know you that I shall kill him, and when he is dead who will know of it? For the boys who serve the wines do not sleep in this house, and to them we can say, Our master is sick, and they will suspect nothing. And as for the visitors who come for entertainment, they never see our master. For do not we have to go to them and sit on their knees and kiss them and coax them until they give us gold. And indeed they little know that our master takes the gold off us when we get behind the screen. Salma agreed with the words of her brother and she said: Verily we should risk all and slay him.

The next day, when the dancing hall was closed for the night, Nasirulla took a mouse he had caught and he threw it in the great jar of wine, which had a neck as large as a wheel, and the mouse swam around in the wine, nor did it want to drown. Then Nasirulla called out to his master: Come and help me, for there is a mouse in the wine. And the Turk grew angry, for he thought: This is some trick of the boy to dip a bowl in the wine and steal some of it. So the Turk came over and he peered into the jar of wine. And as he was looking for the mouse in the jar, Nasirulla caught him a blow on the back of the head with an iron bar, and he fell forward stunned, with his head in the jar. Then Nasirulla called his sister and together they lifted the legs of the Turk and they thrust him completely into the jar of wine. And upside down in the jar of wine the Turk met the Angel of Death. And Nasirulla and Salma took what gold they could find in the house and put it in their pockets. Yet it was not sufficient for them, for they did not know where the Turk kept his main hoard of gold.

The next night the boys who served the wine came to the dancing hall, and Nasirulla said to them: Know you that our master is sick, but you are to take the wine from the tap at the bottom of the jar as is your custom, and you will bring the money to me, for I am acting for our master, until, please God it may be soon, he is recovered and in health.

The boys drew the wine from the tap at the bottom of the jar, and they took it and gave it to the guests who were coming into the dancing hall. Then Nasirulla and Salma went out and they danced in a manner in which they had never danced before. And the Pashas and the Beys were amazed, for never had they seen such dancing, and they said one to the other: Never has the entertainment been so good as it is tonight, and even the wine tastes better and has more body to it.

And after their dance was finished Nasirulla and Salma went out and they sat on the knees of the Pashas and on the knees of the Beys and they kissed them and tickled their ears until they pulled out their bags of gold and they gave them money such as they had never given before. And that night when they closed the dancing hall Nasirulla and his sister counted their money and they said: If we can keep this up for one more week, then we shall have enough money to return to the Caucasus.

The next night the hall was even more crowded than it had been on the first night, for the Pashas and the Beys had told their friends of the excellence of the dancing and the quality of the wine. And again Nasirulla and Salma danced in the most exquisite manner and again they kissed and tickled the ears of the Ottomans and they received even more gold than before. And the noble Pashas and Beys said to each other: The wine at this hall gets better every night, and as for the dancing, there is none like it in the world.

And again on the third night and on the fourth night the dancing was perfect and the wine was getting richer and richer and Nasirulla and Salma collected much gold.

But on the fifth night so many Turkish officers came to the hall that they could not all enter, and they quarrelled one with the other and fought to get in and a noble Bey was killed. And the Wali of Basra was informed of the affair.

On the morning of the sixth day soldiers came to the cabaret and they asked Nasirulla: Where is Jamal Effendi, the owner of this hall? Nasirulla's heart was full of fear and he replied: Verily he has gone out to the market, nor do I know when he will return. Then the Shawish in charge of the soldiers said: We have been commanded by the Wali to confiscate the wine of this hall, because it is said to be of such quality that the officers of the garrison are fighting with each other to get at it. And we have also been ordered to take the dancing boy and the dancing girl who perform here, for they have been inflaming the passions of the garrison. But in future they will only perform before the Wali himself.

Nasirulla's face went as pale as death, and he thought: Now our secret is no longer a secret. But he said to the Shawish: Know you that this wine is the finest wine in the world, but it will spoil unless you have a large number of men to move the jar. The jar must be kept vertical and not shaken, for it is most delicate wine, and you must keep the mouth of the jar tightly sealed, lest the cold air strike the wine and spoil it. Then the Shawish went off to fetch porters to take the jar of wine, and Nasirulla said to his sister: Come, for we cannot delay further. Then Nasirulla and Salma left the hall and they went out into the street, and they took with them their gold.

When Nasirulla and Salma came out into the street the time was day, and they thought: Wherever we go now we will be seen by the people. It is better that we hide until nightfall. So they slipped into a large warehouse which was full of chests of Kuweit of enormous size. And Nasirulla opened one of the largest chests and he found it full of silk, so he emptied out the silk and hid it behind another chest. Then he and Salma got in the chest and he closed the lid, and with his knife he made a small hole that they might breathe air within that chest.

And when they had been some time hidden in the chest, Nasirulla and Salma heard footsteps approaching, and men walked into the vault. And one man said to the other: Have you packed the silks? The other man replied: Master, I have packed them with my own hand in this chest. And he tapped with his hand on the chest in which Nasirulla and Salma were hiding. Then the master of the vault ordered: Rope the chest, and I will return in one hour with the camels. But the servant said: Master, I must fetch the porters to lift this chest before the rope can be passed around it, for alone I cannot lift it. And both the master and the servant left the store.

Salma was trembling with fear, and she said to Nasirulla: Let us escape before they return. But Nasirulla replied: Do not fear, for wherever this chest is going, we will go inside it. For it must be going a long way or they would not rope it, and any place is better for us than Basra. When the Wali finds the body of our master in his wine his brain will boil over even as the milk boils when it is left too long on the fire. But wait you here, and in two minutes I will return with bread and water for this may be a long journey. And Nasirulla opened the box and he ran out into the street and he ran to a shop and he said: Give me bread and dates and cheese and take this gold. And Nasirulla bought a large bag and filled it with bread and dates and cheese, and he bought the largest bottle he could see and he filled it with water and he ran back to his sister, and on the way back he bought two water melons also. And Nasirulla got into the chest and he closed the lid, saying to his sister: Know you that these supplies may have to last us even for weeks, for perchance they are loading this chest on to a ship and sending it to India.

After a time the servant returned with porters, and they lifted the chest and roped it securely. Then they brought a camel and loaded the chest and they set out. And Nasirulla and Salma heard the bells of many more camels and they said: This is no ship. Rather it is a caravan on the road to Baghdad. And for days and days the caravan marched, and at night it halted, and each day Nasirulla and Salma took only a sip of water, and a slice of water melon and a few dates.

And when the days had joined to become a week the water melons were finished, and when the weeks had joined to become a month, the water was finished, and only a few dates and a little cheese remained. And Nasirulla said to his sister: Know you that we were not on the road to Baghdad. Perchance we are on the road to Mecca through Busaiyir, or on the road to Syria by way of the desert. And Salma said: If we do not arrive within three days then I must call out to the camel men that they release us, if only to kill us, for I am dying of thirst.

But the next day they heard around them the sounds of a large city and Nasirulla listened to the swearing and shouting of the people of the streets and he said: The tongue is Turkish. How have we arrived in Turkey without passing through a great city? This must be a special caravan carrying goods for the Sultan himself, that it has been able to halt away from the cities, and supplies of water and food have been sent out to be ready for it in the desert that it be not delayed.

The camels came to a halt and porters came and the great chest in which were Nasirulla and Salma was unloaded and carried by the porters for a long way, and finally it was set down on a stone floor. And Nasirulla and Salma knew not where they were. They heard a man come, and he cut the rope around the box, and he said in Turkish: I will go to summon the ladies that they may see the silks. And his voice was the voice of a eunuch. When the footsteps of the eunuch died away, Nasirulla opened the box and peered out, but there was nobody in sight.

So he and his sister staggered out of the chest, for they could scarcely walk from weakness, and they found themselves in a great hall, the walls of which were covered with marble and rare stones and with mirrors set in silver, and in the centre of the hall a fountain was playing. Nasirulla and Salma went to the fountain and they drank until their stomachs were filled. Then Nasirulla took his sister and said: Let us hide until we can find out what this place is, and how we can get out of it, for I do not suppose that it is closely guarded. And Nasirulla and Salma entered a small chamber which led off the main hall, and they found it crowded with the most beautiful dresses, made of rare cloths, and they were all for women, and there was not a single coat or cloak for a man in that room. Amongst the gowns and the dresses Nasirulla and Salma hid.

Then the eunuch returned to the large hall, and Nasirulla was amazed for behind the eunuch followed hundreds and hundreds of the most beautiful girls, and the eunuch went up to the great chest and threw it open, and he cried: Ladies, see the latest chest of silks and fine cloths. But in the chest was only the skin of two water melons, hundreds of date stones, an empty bottle and a smell of dirt for verily Nasirulla and his sister had not left that box

173

for over a month. And the ladies and the eunuch looked into the box and they were amazed what they saw. And the eunuch said: I will go to order the guards of the Palace to seize the camel men that they may feel the bastinado until they die, for verily they have stolen the cloth which our Lord the Sultan had ordered for the ladies of his imperial harem.

Nasirulla heard the words of the eunuch and his heart stopped through very fear, and he said to his sister: Do you know where we are? We are in the Harem of the Sultan himself, the most closely guarded place in the whole empire of the Ottomans, of which it is said that no man can enter it and no man can depart from it alive, and in this place there are only girls and eunuchs.

Nasirulla turned to the dresses in which they were hiding, and he took a dress which fitted him and he put it on, and his own clothes he hid. Salma also selected a new dress and put it on, for her dress was dirty, and after they had put on the dresses Nasirulla and Salma looked like sisters, nor could anyone who saw him tell that Nasirulla was a boy, for he wore his hair long after the fashion of the dancing boys, and his moustache was not grown.

Then they heard the eunuchs call out: Ladies, come to your food. Nasirulla turned to his sister and he said: Let us go and eat, for we are hungry. And Salma replied: What, shall we go amongst them? Nasirulla said: We will go and eat. There are many hundreds of girls here and two new faces will never be noticed amongst them.

So Nasirulla and Salma went out into the hall, and they went into another hall, which was even larger than the first, and in it was laid out a great feast. And they saw before them a hundred roast sheep, and a hundred roast peacocks, and many hundreds of chickens and ducks and

174

pigeon and doves and partridge and quail, and from every direction hundreds of the most beautiful girls in the world were coming and sitting down to the meal and wine was brought for them by Negro slave girls.

Nasirulla and Salma sat down and ate of the feast until their stomachs were bursting, nor did anyone question who they were. And when all hands were withdrawn from eating, the Chief of the Eunuchs came round and he talked to some of the girls, and he came to Nasirulla and Salma and he said to them: Your faces are new. Were you part of the last present to our Lord? And Salma replied: Verily we are new here, and our desire is to be of service to our Lord and Master. But the eunuch sighed and he said: How can this be? It was different in the days when our master was a young man, though even then he rarely needed more than three hundred girls a year. But now he is old and his beard is white and his eyes are dim and even one girl would be too much for him. Yet we have three thousand in this place, and every month another hundred arrive as presents from the great rulers and governers, and these poor girls are condemned to live unloved and unseen in this vast harem, until they kiss and make love to each other from very sadness of heart.

And Nasirulla was amazed at the words of the eunuch, and he thought: While I am here and until I find a way out of this closely guarded place I will at least comfort some of these poor girls.

On the next day and on the following days Nasirulla examined all the doors and windows of the harem, but they were all guarded by eunuchs armed with swords, nor could anyone pass in or out. And the days lengthened into months, but Nasirulla could find no place unguarded save one, and this was a window which was covered by

176

a grid of iron bars as thick as a man's wrist, and beneath the window was a lake, nor could anyone leave the window without swimming through the lake. And Nasirulla commenced to cut away at the bars, using diamonds and precious stones for the work, of which there was an abundance in the harem. But the cutting of each bar in such a manner that it could not be detected took weeks, and it was long before the work was nearing completion.

One day, just before Nasirulla had finished the cutting of the bars, Salma came to Nasirulla and her face was as pale as death, and she said to him: There is a rumour among the girls, and I believe this rumour to be true, that some eighty of them are become pregnant, and indeed they have children in their stomachs, and it is known that these cannot be the children of our Lord the Sultan. And after a short time these children will become known and they will become apparent even to the Chief Eunuch himself, and when that happens there will be such investigations and such floggings and tortures and executions that the fountain in this harem will spray only blood. And when Nasirulla heard the words of his sister he turned faint with fear, and he thought: Can such great consequences come from such little cause?

Then Nasirulla took his sister and they went to the window and they finished the cutting of the remaining bar. And in the lake beneath the window Nasirulla saw two naked boys, who were in the sixteenth year of their life, and they were swimming and amusing themselves in the water. Nasirulla said to his sister: We must get these boys out of the way and we must steal their clothes, for if we dive now into the water they may raise the alarm, and if we land from the lake in wet clothes, then we shall attract attention. And verily we cannot walk through the city in the silken dresses of the harem.

Salma realised the truth of her brother's words, and she saw the clothes of the boys, which were lying safe and dry on the far bank of the lake. So Salma called out to the boys, and they saw the faces of two beautiful girls at the window for they knew not that Nasirulla was a boy, and they swam over to beneath the window, and Salma said to them: We are two and you are two, come up here and play.

And the boys replied: How can we do this when that window is covered by bars as thick as a man's arm? And is not that the Imperial Harem, the penalty for entering which is death by torture? Salma said: Do not fear. Just swarm up the wall and we will loosen the bars, nor will anyone see you, for the eunuchs never come to this window, as it is considered secure. And when you are inside we will hide you in a small chamber where none can see you, then let us amuse ourselves for an hour, and then you can return to the lake and to your clothes. And the boys thought: Verily, there is no danger, and what a jest it will be to go into the Sultan's harem itself.

So they clambered out of the water and up the wall, and they were in a naked condition. Nasirulla and Salma loosened the bars and let the boys in and led them to a small chamber which had only one door and no windows, and they said: Here we can amuse ourselves unseen. And Nasirulla and Salma said to the boys: Wait here while we look around the corners and see that the eunuchs are sleeping peacefully. But when Nasirulla and Salma were outside the door, they shut it and drove home a great bolt which secured that door from the outside, and the two boys were left prisoners in that room.

Then Nasirulla and Salma stripped off their clothes and they dived into the water and swam over the lake to the clothes of the boys, and Nasirulla had tied around his waist a rope to which was tied much gold and rare jewels. And Nasirulla and Salma reached the clothes of the boys and they put them on and they became as two boys, for their long hair they wrapped in the turbans of the boys.

And as for the boys they sat in the small chamber and they said: How sportive are these girls, for they have locked the door on us. This is indeed a fine joke. But the minutes passed and passed and the boys became cold, for they were wet and naked, and they began to fear, for they thought: This place is the Sultan's harem, and it is no place to be caught in through some foolish girlish trick. But the girls did not return and the boys sat naked and shivering with fear and an hour passed.

And out in the main courtyard of the harem the Chief Eunuch sat with his assistants who were not guarding the doors and he was watching some of the girls washing at a fountain. And he said to his comrades: Are not some of the figures of the girls changing, or do my eyes play me tricks? And the eunuchs answered: Verily your thoughts are our thoughts, and we have also seen many girls lately who are red-eyed from weeping. There is truly some matter here which requires investigation.

Then the Chief Eunuch sent for a wise woman and she came and examined the girls, and she said to the Eunuch: Verily these girls are blessed with children. The Chief Eunuch was horrified at the words of the wise woman, and he thought: Who can be the father of these children? It cannot be the Sultan our master, nor can he be from us the eunuchs, and apart from us there are only girls here, nor can a man enter this place. So he ordered two of the

179

eunuchs to take one of the girls and they tied her up by her thumbs to the beam of the ceiling, and the Chief Eunuch said: There shall you remain until your thumbs pull out from your hands or until you tell us the truth of this matter. And the girl stayed for twenty minutes until she screamed out in agony, and she said: Know you that by magic, in the night, one of the girls in this harem becomes a boy, and she is one of the two Circassian sisters who are so much alike, and though in the daytime she is as a girl, yet at night she is a boy, and there is no doubt about this whatever.

The Chief Eunuch ordered the eunuchs: Go and fetch me the two Circassian sisters who are so alike. And they went off and they searched, but they returned and said: We cannot find them. The Chief Eunuch ordered them to go again and to search every room and every chamber in the great building of the harem. And they went and they searched and searched and they came to the chamber in which were the two naked boys, and they opened the door of that chamber and they found them within it, and they took them and chained them and brought them in front of the Chief Eunuch.

And the two boys wept and implored mercy from the Chief Eunuch, but he showed them no mercy. He commanded that they be tied by their thumbs to the beam of the ceiling, and that thing was done to them. He then ordered the eunuchs to flog them with whips until their lives were ended, for he thought: How can I show mercy when my own life is now in the most terrible danger?

And when the two boys were dead, the wise woman came to the Chief Eunuch and said: Verily eighty of the girls in this harem are in a condition of pregnancy. The heart of the Chief Eunuch stopped beating from very horror, and he thought: Now my royal master will end my life. And he thought and thought and a way appeared open to him, and he said to himself: I will announce this to the Sultan in open court, then through very shame he cannot confess that he is not able to have fathered these children.

So the next morning the Chief Eunuch went to the Royal Diwan, and there in the presence of the great ministers and generals and the distinguished people of the country he announced in a high voice: Majesty, eighty of the ladies of your harem are blessed with children. And those sitting in the court were amazed, for the beard of the Sultan was white and his eyes were dim and he dribbled down his beard. And the Sultan said nothing to the Chief Eunuch. However, when the court was over the Sultan retired to a private chamber and he sent for his secretary, whom he trusted, and he said: Kill the Chief of my Eunuchs and take his body and bury it and let it be known in the court that he has died of sickness. And the secretary obeyed the orders of his master the Sultan.

And as for Nasirulla and Salma, when they had put on the clothes of the boys, they went into the city, and Nasirulla purchased weapons and two horses of the finest stock and six baggage ponies and they loaded them with supplies and they set out that very night for their own country, nor did they desire to linger in the lands of the Turks, and after many weeks of travel they arrived in safety. And Nasirulla married a wife and he gave his sister Salma in marriage, and when in the winter evenings he used to go to the wineshop and drink with his friends, he would say to them: Know you that I have eighty children. But they did not believe his words.

THE STORY OF SHEIKH MIZEIL

EL QURNACHI, A MAN OF A
NOBLE FAMILY, THOUGH HIS
LANDS WERE POOR

ONCE in the days of the Ottomans there lived in Baghdad a man of an ancient and noble family named Sheikh Mizeil el Qurnachi, and he lived in a great house by the banks of the Tigris. Yet his estates had been reduced by the taxation and oppression of the Ottomans, and his crops spoiled by locust and by flood until he was reduced to poverty.

So he lived in his house with his only daughter without a single servant or a single slave, nor was there any furniture or silver left in his house, for he had sold all to buy food. Yet the house he could not sell, for it would be shameful for him to do so, since it was the house of his ancestors.

The name of his daughter was Nura. She was in the seventeenth year of her life, yet none had asked for her in marriage, for since there were no servant girls to gossip about her beauty, the boys of great and noble families had not even heard of her. Else surely their sleep would have been troubled by her description, for her hair was as black as the Shatt el Arab on a clear winter's night, and her eyes were as the stars which glisten in its waters, her skin was as golden as the desert sand when tinged by the first rosy red rays of dawn, her back was as supple as the reeds before the wind, and her thighs and breasts had the softness of the feather quilt which allures the tired traveller.

So one day Nura went to her father and she said to him: O my beloved father, my state is thus and thus. Shall I be forever a cook in your household or shall I be the mother of noble sons? And Sheikh Mizeil grieved much at the words of his daughter, and his heart was sad. And on the nights of the full moon Nura would go out on the roof of their great house, and speak to the moon and ask the question:

183

O Moon, you shine on youths and maidens,
Where is my lover, where is he,
He who will love me with the strongest love?
And the moon, ashamed at the waste of such beauty,
would hide behind the nearest cloud.

And one day Sheikh Mizeil came on his daughter and
found her weeping, so he took her hand and said to her:
O my little one, know you that we are more unfortunate
than the poorest beggar of the City of Peace. For were I
of the general run of men, I could work as a clerk, or as a
washerman, or even as a porter or sweeper, and so gain
a little money. But our name is a known name and it is
shameful for me to work, or that any should know of our
poverty. Therefore starvation faces us, and it is in my mind
that we should cut the veins in our wrists, and so depart,
but first take you this the last of my gold and make yourself a dress fit for a woman of our family, that when the
neighbours come in and lay out our bodies for burial they
may find you dressed as befits our dignity.

So Nura put on her veil and she took the gold coins
from her father, though the tears flowed from her eyes.
And Nura went to the market and she went to the sellers
of fine stuffs. And she bought the finest silk. Yet there was
still some of the money unspent, so she went into a great
shop, thinking: I will buy sequins with the last of the
money and cover the dress with sequins, that in death they
who find me will remember me. So she went to the
merchant, who was named Jassim, and she asked of him
for sequins, and he showed her jar after jar filled with the
finest sequins of every known colour, and also of colours
that are no longer remembered. And she gazed at the
sequins and she gazed at her silk that she might exactly
match its delicate colour. And while comparing the

184

colours she let her veil slip from her face. Yet such was her concentration that she did not know that her beauty was exposed.

And the merchant Jassim gazed at her, and his gaze was the gaze of a jackal which looks at a dying gazelle, for Jassim was among those who desire the despoiling of girls, and his thoughts were evil thoughts. And he looked at Nura's face and he looked at the cloth of her cloak and her veil and he thought: She is not rich, yet her face is beyond compare, but who can dispense with caution? First I must discover her station and know if she has any brother or father to avenge her honour. And since he did not know her, or from whence she came, he thought of a cunning ruse. When she bought the sequins and ordered fifty mithkals of them, he weighed them out and packed them in a paper bag, but with his little finger he pierced the paper of the bag and left in it a small hole. So when Nura paid for the sequins and took the bag, it left a trail of sequins. Yet such was Nura's distraction and grief that she noticed it not.

Nura left the shop and returned to her father's house, and at a safe distance behind her followed Jassim. Nor was he in any doubt about the path she had taken, for on the ground lay a clear trail of glittering sequins. And through and about narrow passages and side turnings of Baghdad he followed her, though he could not see her, until he came to a great teakwood door studded with brass. And though the door was closed, he knew that she had entered, for the doorstep was sprinkled with sequins and there the trail ended. So Jassim asked and questioned the poor people of the street concerning the house with the teakwood door, and they replied: That is Qasr Qurnachi, and formerly it was a great and wealthy house, for they used to slaughter ten sheep every day to feed the poor, but now the old sheikh lives there with his only daughter, without any servant or slave, nor does anybody else go in, nor does anybody else come out.

And Jassim thought and pondered, and he said to himself: Qurnachi is a great name. I would be unwise to meddle with that girl, for her father would surely kill me. Rather should I take a better course. Why should I not marry her? Then not only could I enjoy her beauty without fear, but I could also remark to my friends in the coffee-house: My latest wife is a model housekeeper. Of course, you know she is a Qurnachi. And then they will eye me with the eye of respect and my sons will mingle with those of noble blood, and since the sheikh is so poor I will offer him a handsome price and he will accept.

So on the next day Jassim the merchant called at the house of Sheikh Mizeil el Qurnachi, and he knocked on the great door, for he was not acquainted with that conduct which is seemly. And Sheikh Mizeil opened the door himself and bade him welcome and entrance, for the Sheikh was a true Arab. And he said to him: I am honoured by your visit, respected merchant, but pardon me for the poorness of your reception, for I gave all my servants and staff permission to go to their homes and take a day's rest. Nor have I anyone here to prepare for you food or coffee, so pardon my rudeness, and pray tell me your name and your business with speed, that you may not linger in discomfort.

And Jassim replied, and his reply was an abrupt reply, lacking in dignity and form, and he said: Noble sheikh, as for my name, it is Jassim Kuweity, and I own the great cloth shop. And as for my business, it is marriage, for I hear you have a daughter, and as for the sum, I will pay

186

one hundred thousand gold liras. Sheikh Mizeil was
amazed at the words of the merchant and his face went
black, and he said: You have lost your way. Are you
looking for a brothel? I know your name and I have heard
of you. Is it not said that your grandfather sold milk?
Does then the vulture mate with the peacock? Were you
other than a donkey's droppings you would not live after
making this suggestion. As it is, I will give you a lesson in
respect even as it is taught to slaves.

And Sheikh Mizeil seized Jassim in a grip of iron and he
commenced beating the merchant about the head and
ears with his riding-switch until the blood flowed. And
when Sheikh Mizeil was satisfied with beating Jassim he
took him and cast him out into the dust. And Nura saw
these events from a window of the inner courtyard, and
she was amazed, thinking: Was not that the merchant
from whom I bought the sequins? How then did he know
our house? Then Nura, for she was a clever girl, remembered that the bag of sequins had been half empty on her
arrival, and she looked out of the door and saw that the
threshold was still sprinkled with sequins, and she thought:
This was the stratagem of the lustful merchant.

And as for Jassim, he picked himself up from the dusty
street and walked back to his shop, and his heart was full
of anger and the desire for revenge. And he pondered:
How can I bring this old maniac to ruin, he who has
dared to treat me in this manner, he who has not even
enough copper coins to put together to make a pair? And
he returned to his shop and he went to his treasure chest
and he opened it and he counted out ten thousand gold
liras. He put the coins in a handkerchief of the finest silk,
and he left his shop and he went to the house of the
Turkish pasha, Commandant of Police, and he entered

and saluted the officer and he spoke to him after this fashion: O Your Honour, how much have I heard of your wise administration and your great munificence and your benevolent hospitality? I have come in your service to offer you a humble present, which I request you to honour me by expending in your great charitable and hospitable fashion. And Jassim placed the handkerchief of coins on the table, and the Turk eyed the present and saw that it was heavy, and he bade Jassim be seated and he ordered coffee.

And after suitable and polite conversation, Jassim said: O your Excellency the Pasha, I desire to warn you of a most dangerous plot and a devilish intrigue directed against even the Caliph himself, and the prime mover who has given birth to this foul conspiracy is none other than an Arab landowner named Sheikh Mizeil el Qurnachi, cursed be his brood and sour be his food.

And the Commandant listened to the words of Jassim, and he summoned an officer and ordered: Take soldiers and go to Qasr Qurnachi and seize the Sheikh and fetter him. Then take him and chain him to the wall in the jail, for he is a danger to the State and an investigation must be made and an enquiry directed into the sedition which he has plotted.

Nura and her father were sitting in their house when they heard the tramp of horses and a thunderous knocking on the great door, and Sheikh Mizeil opened the door to the soldiers to enquire their business. But as for Nura, she turned and hid herself in the great house, thinking: Should these Turks see me, then should I not remain a maiden. And she saw the Turks seize her father and fetter him and lead him away, and she thought: This is the work of the merchant Jassim. And when the soldiers had taken her

188

father and gone away Nura wept and sobbed until her heart was nearly broken.

But she was a true Arab girl, so after a time she dried her tears and she ran to a cupboard which contained old clothes, and she took the clothes of a page boy, which had remained there from the days when Sheikh Mizeil had many servants and pages, and she cast off her clothes and she put on the clothes of a boy, and she took a riding-switch and put on a headcloth and aqal. And she left the house, thinking: Should I remain, then Jassim will seek me and find me. Yet her feet were bare, for she could find no boy's shoes to fit her feet. And she walked out into the street and away, not knowing where to go or where to find refuge. And she thought: I will go from Baghdad and go to the great tribes, for the people of the city lack generosity. But he who goes to the tribes, him they feed and shelter, and there I will devise a plan to save my father. So she walked and walked and went out from Baghdad and took the road to Basra, and she walked for many hours on the dusty road, and all who saw her thought that she was a boy.

And those that passed Nura on the road saluted her and she returned their salutation. And Nura walked and walked until the sun was in the west and her feet were torn and bleeding from the roughness of the road, when she saw before her a great cavalcade of horsemen. At their head rode a young Sheikh, whose face was as the full moon and whose bearing was as noble as a sword blade, and as they came up to Nura and passed her the riders saluted the walker and their greeting was returned, and the young Sheikh glanced at Nura, whom he thought to be a beautiful boy. And the Sheikh, who was none other than Aqab er Rejab, rode on, returning his glance to the ground after the manner of sheikhs who are pondering on affairs of state and high matters.

And after he had ridden on for ten minutes after passing the boy, the Sheikh urged his horse and cantered out away from his followers, calling one of his men, who was the chief of his trackers, to accompany him. And Sheikh Aqab er Rejab turned to that wise tracker Abood el Matrood, he who could tell from her tracks how many weeks a she camel had been in foal, and he spoke to him and said: Ya Abood, cast your eyes on the ground and tell me what you see there written concerning the moon-faced boy we passed not ten minutes ago. And Abood el Matrood replied and said: O son of Rejab, I am astonished, for my eyes saw the form of a boy, yet these footprints are the footprints of a girl. For that is not the shape of a boy's foot, nor is this stride a boy's stride, and also this girl is sore tired, nor is she used to walking barefoot. Aqab spoke and said: Your thoughts are my thoughts, but let this remain a secret. Ride back to the girl, and offer her my hospitality for the night, for the sun is in the west and we must camp, and we are travellers and she is a traveller. Yet disclose not to her that we know her to be a girl.

Then while Abood el Matrood rode back to carry out the orders of the Sheikh, Aqab er Rejab halted his men and ordered them to pitch the black tents, and to prepare the evening meal. And Abood returned with Nura, and the Sheikh asked her: O comrade of the road, who are you and where are you going? Nura replied and said: As for my name, it is Nuri, and I know not where I am going, for I am only a poor servant boy, and my master is imprisoned, and I seek refuge from oppression. And when the great hair tent was pitched the Sheikh questioned Nura until she had related the whole story to him, only

190

she pretended to be Sheikh Mizeil el Qurnachi's page boy rather than his daughter. And she said: As for Sheikh Mizeil's beautiful daughter, I know not what became of her. Perhaps she has thrown herself in the river to escape from shame. And the Sheikh spoke and said: This affair shall be my affair, for I know Sheikh Mizeil's name, and I think there is some blood connection between us and that we are distant cousins, and does not the poet say:

A man has cousins,
They are like his wings.
Can then the hawk,
Fly without wings?

And when the food was eaten Sheikh Aqab ordered that the page boy be given a hair tent of his own to sleep in, and he whispered to Abood el Matrood: Guard her well in the night. Then the Sheikh sat in his own tent, passing his rosary through his fingers, thinking: How can I overcome the sequin seller and release Mizeil from the Turks, that I may earn the love of this girl? And by the time that the Star of Dawn was clear he had formed a plan. And when the first glow of dawn was in the East the Sheikh ordered the striking of the camp, and they took to the road, and as for their destination, it was Baghdad.

And on the morning of the second day the merchant Jassim rose from his bed and left his house and went to his shop as was his custom, and he called his assistants and slaves and shop boys and asked them and said: Have you yet found this runaway girl, daughter of the traitor Mizeil, and did you search for her throughout the night? And they replied: Master, we have searched every quarter in Baghdad, yet we cannot find her. Yet there is a matter of which we desire to acquaint you, for it fills us with fear, and that is that last night after you had left the shop there came a man, and his face was hidden in his headcloth, and his tongue the tongue of the tribes, and he questioned us, asking: Is this the shop of the merchant Jassim? At what time does he come and at what time does he go? Where does he live and where does he eat? Where does he sit and where does he sleep? And the merchant Jassim liked not the words of his servants.

After an hour or so spent in trade and profit Jassim left his shop and went to the coffee-house as was his custom, that he might meet his friends and pass half an hour in the pleasures of conversation. And when he rose from the coffee-shop to return to his shop he saw that the road was sprinkled with sequins, and the trail of sequins led back to his own shop. And he was amazed at what he saw, and he felt in his pockets, thinking: Perhaps I put a bag of sequins in my pocket, and they have leaked out and made this trail. But he felt in his pockets and there were no sequins there.

And at the time of noon he left his shop and went to his house, and while he was seated at his food his slave boy ran in and said: Master, your bag of sequins is leaking. And Jassim went to the door of his house and he saw that a trail of sequins covered the path he had taken from his shop. So after he had fed and was satisfied, Jassim left his house, thinking: I will go to the river bank that I may see who is following me and sprinkling sequins behind me, for there there is an open space, and I can look behind me.

So Jassim walked out by the river bank, and he kept glancing behind him, yet nobody was in sight. And he walked in a great circle through the palm trees, yet he saw no son of Adam. And while returning to the town he recrossed the path he had taken and saw that it was sprinkled with sequins. And when he saw this, he ran and ran back to the town and to his house, though he was a portly merchant.

And he went into his house and ordered his servants to bring him the dress of a woman, and they brought it, and he disguised himself, thinking: I will disguise myself as a woman and go to my brother's house and hide there, that I may escape from evil. And he came out of his house cloaked in a woman's cloak and veil, so that nobody could recognise him, and he walked to his brother's house at the other end of Baghdad, and knocked on the door and asked to see his brother. He was admitted and when he was in his brother's chamber he disclosed himself to him.

And while he was relating his situation to his brother there came a knock at the door and a servant cried out: Master, tell the old lady who is with you that her bag of sequins is leaking, for there is a trail of sequins leading right up to our threshold. And Jassim was amazed at what he heard, for he knew not that he was being followed by Abood el Matrood, whom no disguise could fool, since he recognised people by their footprints on the ground. Then Jassim and his brother ran out of the room and they saw that the words of the servant were true, for the threshold was sprinkled with sequins and a trail of sequins led away on the path taken by Jassim dressed as a woman. Then the brother turned to Jassim and said: Fear nothing and dread not death, for you will sleep here tonight and I will stand to guard you as you sleep with a drawn sword in my hand.

So when night came the brother of Jassim ordered all his servants to arm themselves and he posted them at the doors and windows of the house, so that not even a mouse could come in or go out. Then Jassim lay down to sleep on his brother's bed, and his brother stood on guard beside him with a drawn sword. And Jassim slept and his heart was free from fear. But in the morning when he awoke his heart stopped and he turned faint from very fear, for the sheets of the bed were sprinkled with sequins, and his brother lay dead on the floor in a great pool of blood, and the blood of his brother was spangled with sequins.

So Jassim leapt from his bed and he ran from the room and from the house dressed as he was in his dress of the night, and as he went out he saw that all the slaves and all sentries who had guarded the doors in the night lay dead in pools of blood, spangled with sequins. So Jassim ran from his brother's house through the streets of the City of Peace, nor was he aware that those in the streets and the common people glanced in surprise at the portly merchant running in his nightshift. So Jassim ran and ran, and his destination was his shop.

But as Jassim drew near his shop he saw a great crowd there collected and he heard much shouting and commotion, and as he came up to his shop puffing and panting and out of breath his shop assistants and boys and apprentices caught hold of him and cried: O you in whose footsteps fall sequins, give us our pay and release us and let us depart in peace, for we cannot serve one accursed. And they led him into the shop, and he saw that the whole shop was sprinkled with sequins, and the watchman of the night lay dead in pools of blood, spangled with sequins, and on his great desk was a message in verse, written in blood sparkling with sequins, and it was written in Arabic and it read:

When Mizeil dies you die
When Mizeil is saved, you are saved.

So Jassim dressed himself in suitable attire and he left

his shop and he went to the house of the Commandant of the Ottoman Police, and he entered and saluted the officer and said: O Your Honour the Commandant, I have come to right a wrong and to replace injustice with justice. For I have discovered that I made a most foolish and careless mistake concerning Sheikh Mizeil el Qurnachi. He was not plotting sedition. Rather, he was praising the noble Ottoman Government and praying for the long life and prosperity of our lord, His Majesty the Caliph. Yet I mistook his words. So please show your famous clemency and mercy and release this gentle old sheikh.

But the Commandant of Police frowned and he spoke and his voice was lacking in mercy and he said: How can this be? For the date of execution of the treacherous sheikh is already fixed and ordained and reports have been made and submitted to high officers and ministers and even to the Caliph our Lord and Sultan concerning the plot which our watchful and vigilant police have detected and brought to light.

And Jassim replied and said: As for the noble old sheikh, he is indeed innocent. But there is a cloth merchant named Mizeil who was verily involved in the plot which Your Honour has detected, and his shop is near to my shop. Therefore let him be arrested and justice done, and this information is the true information. And as for me, pardon my carelessness and my error, for the names are similar, and though Your Honour has mentioned no punishment for me, yet I see that my mistake has caused trouble to Your Excellency, and I desire to punish myself. Therefore I go now to fetch one hundred thousand gold liras which I desire to pay you as a fine, for can carelessness go unpunished, should it inconvenience a high officer of state? So the Commandant agreed to the words of Jassim and he summoned an officer and ordered that Sheikh Mizeil el Qurnachi be released, and the traitor Mizeil the Merchant arrested and brought to justice.

So Sheikh Mizeil came out of the prison a free man, and he went to his house, and his daughter Nura joined him there. Yet her heart was sad, for she was filled with great love for the noble Sheikh Aqab er Rejab, and she thought: He thinks me a boy, therefore will he not desire me, and I cannot discover myself to him, for I am an honourable girl. Therefore she was amazed and astonished when she saw a venerable sayyid of great dignity come in state to her father, and her father, after conversation with the sayyid, came to her and asked: Do you consent, O my eyes, to be taken in marriage by the noble Sheikh Aqab er Rejab, the father of a thousand swords? And Nura said to her father: I consent. And Nura thought: How did Aqab know my sex? And that night she went on to the roof of her house and she spoke to the moon and she said:

O Moon, you shine on youths and maidens
I have a lover, there is One
One who will love me with the strongest love.
And the moon smiled and did not hide behind a cloud.

As for the happiness and bliss of Nura and Aqab er Rejab, that I cannot describe to you, for since you did not see them together you would not comprehend my words. But if you ask me concerning the merchant Jassim, and if you question me concerning his affairs, then I will tell you that he was much reduced in wealth, for the Turks took from him much gold. Yet his lust and desire for young girls was not diminished, and he arranged to marry the daughter of a poor Persian milk-seller, a girl as beautiful as a gazelle, and since the price he paid for her was a large price, and since the girl was weeping and sobbing and crying out: Can then my slender body be touched by that fat old merchant?—for these reasons and to comfort her, her father gave her some of the gold, and he said to her: Go to the bazaar and to the Mistress of Dressmakers, and let her make a marriage dress such as has never been known before.

And the girl dried her tears and she took her sisters and aunts and her friends and she went to the Mistress of Dressmakers, and she said: I desire such a dress as has never been known before on any marriage bed. And there was much whispering and conference and discussion, and finally the Mistress of Dressmakers whispered her idea to one of the girls, and the girl whispered to another girl, and in this manner they all heard the idea, and as they heard it they clapped their hands and cried: O pretty idea, O happy thought, O lovely device.

And on the night of the marriage when the feast was ended Jassim took his bride into the bedroom and he removed her cloak, and she was dressed in a lovely dress of shimmering silk, lovely against her golden skin, and Jassim was pleased to see that the dress was pure and untouched by any decoration or frill, nor was there on it a single sequin. And he laid his bride on the bed and he removed her dress and she was clad in an ataq and bag trousers of the finest silk, and he removed her ataq and exposed her lovely breasts, but when he came to remove her bag trousers he found that the knot was a tight knot, nor could he untie it.

But his hands were eager hands, nor would they brook delay. So he took hold of her bag trousers and gave a great pull, and the waist band broke, but as it broke there was a shower of sequins, and the lovely skin of his bride was sparkling with sequins, the sheets of the bed were

198

spangled with sequins, and there were even sequins in his hair. For the clever dressmaker had tied paper bags of sequins all around the waist band, and had sown them to a cord around the girl's waist. Yet the girl did not understand why Jassim ran from the room dressed only in his vest, and with words coming from his mouth which were not words of reason. And in the morning they found him wandering naked in the street, making noises such as a dog makes, so they chained him and took him to the House of the Mad.

THE STORY OF DAOUD THE

CAMEL AND OF HIS MISFOR-
TUNES

ONCE in Mosul there was an Arab, a Christian, named Daoud es Suleiman, and he worked as a goldsmith in the market, and all the ladies of Mosul would visit his shop and order from him bangles of gold, studded with pearls, and earrings and necklaces of gold and rare jewels. So his trade was great and he lived in wealth and comfort with his wife, a girl of perfect form and beauty, and his life was a life of happiness and ease.

And one day he was sitting in his shop at the time of the evening prayer, and he was putting away his gold and rare jewels in his iron chest, and his shop boy was closing the shutters, and he was preparing for the coming of night, when there came to his shop a girl, and she was veiled as are the girls of the towns, and she was sobbing and weeping, and she spoke to Daoud, and as for her voice, it was the voice of a nightingale. She gave to Daoud a necklace of gold and pearls and rings and earrings of gold and rare stones, and she said: O Nazarene, take these my jewels and give me money, for I am in need and urgent haste. So Daoud took the jewels and he examined the stones, and he rubbed the gold with acid and weighed it until he was satisfied.

Then he turned to her and said: Know you, O lady, that these jewels are worth five thousand liras and not less, yet I have not so much money in my shop, for I only keep here jewellery. Therefore come you here tomorrow at the rising of the sun, and I will take your jewels and give you money. But the girl burst out sobbing and weeping in a manner to tear the heart, and she said: O merchant, give me the money now, else my life be ended and my lover destroyed.

And Daoud questioned her and asked her concerning her affairs, and she replied, saying: Kind merchant, know you that I am the daughter of a great family, and their name is a respected and feared name, and I was a model of virtue. Yet it so happened and came about that I was walking in the street and I saw a youth, and his face had the beauty of a gazelle, and at that very instant a puff of wind, a wicked, naughty puff of wind, blew aside my veil, and our eyes met, and their meeting was as the union of two streams. And when I walked on I saw that he was following me, and my erring feet led me to the date gardens outside the town, nor could I control the course they took. And there we met and had speech and conversation, I and my lover, and there we used to meet every day. Yet now through some foul slander my father and my brothers are aware of the affair. They have not killed me; they seek to discover the name of my lover that he may share my fate. Therefore have they kept silent and they let me go my way, but they follow me everywhere, that when I meet my lover they may recognise him and kill him. But through a trick I have escaped from them since half an hour ago. Therefore give me the money that I may find my lover and flee the town.

Then Daoud spoke and said: If you desire the money now, there is only one way. Come with me to a money-changer. He will give me the money, since I am known to him. Then I will give it to you.

And the girl agreed to the words of Daoud. So he closed his shop, and they walked together through the streets in the direction of the bankers' market. And as they were turning a corner in the narrow street they met two men, and as she saw them the girl screamed and turned and she ran away with the speed of the gazelle, and the men cried: That is our sister with her lover. And they came up and seized Daoud and looked at his face, saying: This is the Christian goldsmith. We know his house and we know his shop and we know his name. And as for Daoud, he shook with fear and he said: Verily I am innocent, and as for your sister I have never seen her or known her or heard her name. But one of the brothers struck Daoud with his riding-switch, saying: It is seemly that those about to die should meet that angel who is appointed to take their souls with dignity, with patience, and with gladness, for he is God's messenger. Therefore, O smith, cease from unmanly pleading and go you to your house, and there prepare your affairs and settle your business and make your peace with the One God. And, if it be the will of God, tomorrow at the time of the dawn prayer, you will meet him whose coming all await and all expect, for he comes to every man at his appointed time, nor can a coward avoid him, nor can a brave man escape him. And as for us, we know your house and we know your shop, and we will be beside you at that time.

Daoud returned to his house, and his hands were shaking and tears flowed from his eyes, and he entered and embraced his wife and acquainted her with his state. And her tears mingled with his tears and her sobs echoed his sobs and they spent an hour in lamentation and in grief. And after they were exhausted with sobbing and weeping, the girl, the wife of Daoud, spoke and she said: O my lover, go from here and go to another city, for only in this way can your life be spared. Does not a caravan march from here at the sixth hour of night, for the time is summer? Wrap you all our store of gold and jewels in a handkerchief and depart.

So Daoud wrapped his wealth in a handkerchief and he covered his face with his headcloth and donned his cloak and left his house and he went to the serai and he joined the caravan. It marched at the sixth hour, and its destination was Baghdad.

And when they had been two days on the road, and the caravan was traversing the territories of the Shammar of the Jezira, they came on Bedawin, raiders, mounted on horses and on fine camels, and the riders rode up to the caravan and cried: Who be you, where do you go, from whence do you come, and by whose permission? And the Turkish officers and soldiers who were guarding the caravan cried out: We march by order of the Government. Make way! Make way! And the raiders shouted: Are the Ottomans, then, a Government? Know you that we are the Government here, and this is our customs post, and here we levy excise. And as for the caravan, we permit it to proceed when we have levied the tax, and as for the soldiers, we disarm them and permit them to return from whence they have come, but they shall go on foot.

And the Turkish officers saw that the tribesmen were many, well mounted and well armed, so they ordered their soldiers to lay down their arms, crying: Moslems! Spare our lives! And the tribesmen said: Our pledge is given. And the Turks dismounted from their horses and turned back on foot towards Mosul, and their arms they left on the ground.

Then the tribesmen cried out: Merchants, unload your camels and open your loads, that we may inspect the merchandise and levy the tax. And the merchants and camel men made the camels kneel and commenced unloading them. And Daoud was standing by a load of copper vessels and he saw that they were copper water pots of that shape which has a narrow neck through which the hand cannot pass and which has a long straight spout, and which has only one use, and that is known to you. For is it not used for cleansing in the closet? And Daoud thought after this manner: Why should I not slip my jewels into one of these pots, for do the Bedawin use these water pots? They will never levy a tax on these goods.

So Daoud took his bag of gold and jewels and made it long and thin and he slipped it down the neck of a water pot, nor did any see him do it. And the tribesmen came and inspected the loads, crying: Merchants, the tax is half to us and half to you, for you failed to notify us of your coming, that we might come to some other agreement. And they inspected the loads and from each load they took half and left half. And verily those Bedawin took those things that their hearts desired, of silks and linens and Mosul cloth, of rugs and carpets, of sugar and tobacco, of watches and clocks, of saddles and blankets and almonds and honey, of threads and needles and cheeses and charcoal, and they even took an umbrella. But when they came to the load of water pots they laughed and said: We permit these goods to pass exempt and tax free.

And men from amongst the men, the raiders, searched each of the merchants and took from them their purses and opened them, saying: These gold coins bear the cipher of the Ottomans and are confiscated, for we do not permit their circulation in our land. And they came on Daoud and searched him, but they found with him neither goods not gold, so they questioned him, saying: Merchant, where are your goods and where is your wealth? And Daoud replied, saying: I am not a wealthy merchant. I am only a poor coppersmith making enough for my needs, and I go to Baghdad where my mother is sick, and not for purposes of trade. And they took him and led him away, saying: O coppersmith in the fine linen thob, come with us and we will give you food enough for your needs, and may God heal your mother.

And when the Bedawin were finished with the caravan they permitted it to depart, but as for Daoud, they kept him, and he watched the load of copper water pots march away, and in one of the pots was his treasure. And Daoud remained with the Bedawin, even with the Shammar, for many weeks. They fed him with food, but they made him load the camels and unload the camels, and lift and carry the hair tents and heavy loads, and they made him clean the dishes and cooking pots, and on the march they made him walk with the sheep, nor did they permit him to ride. And each evening at sunset they said to him: Were you only a wealthy merchant and not a poor coppersmith you could proceed to Baghdad, after payment of the tax. What a pity that you have to stay here and labour, and may God heal your sick mother. And one evening when he was exhausted from labour in the heat of the day, Daoud cast himself at the feet of the Sheikh, crying: Merciful Sheikh, punish me if you must, for I deceived you. I was indeed wealthy and had with me much gold and precious stones, but I hid my wealth from your tax-gatherers in a water pot. But it marched away with the caravan, and now since many weeks are past, I may never find my treasure again. And the Sheikh laughed much at the words of Daoud, and he said: O Nazarene, your luck is faint and weak, for you have indeed fallen into misfortune. You have less chance of finding that water pot in the City of Peace than of recovering a dirhem dropped in a sandstorm. I permit you to depart and I postpone the payment of the tax. But should you find your water pot, I command you to pay a tax of one copper fils to my agent in

Baghdad, and his name is such and such, for I desire to be acquainted with the outcome of this affair. Then the Sheikh gave Daoud five gold liras and a fine horse and he permitted him to depart.

And Daoud rode away from the Shammar of the Jezira and they wished him God's safety. And after many days on the road he came to Baghdad, and he entered the city and he found a lodging at the house of a friend, like him a Christian from Mosul. And he sold the horse for a good price, and in the morning of the second day he went to the market of copper vessels, thinking: I must be careful not to reveal my object, else many will search for that which is lost, and amongst so many seekers I may not be the finder.

So Daoud wandered through the bazaars and markets, yet did not see the merchant who was the owner of the load of water pots. And the day passed, and another day passed, and a week passed and a month passed, and on each day Daoud wandered through the markets. Yet he did not see that face which amongst all faces he most desired to see. When he had despaired of success and he was sitting in a coffee-house considering his fate a man came up and saluted him, saying: Were you not of that caravan robbed by the Shammar, may their mothers be despoiled, and were you not led away a prisoner? And Daoud looked up and he saw the owner of the load of water pots. So Daoud bade him be seated and he ordered tea.

And after conversation and enquiries of health, Daoud asked the merchant: Have you still that load of water pots? For I am in mind to buy it, since my business is poor, and I will peddle that load from house to house that I may make a little profit. But the merchant replied, saying: As for the water pots, I opened a stall and sold them all, and I sold at a loss, since I had no money left for food or for the expenses of my house. And Daoud said: Tell me, then, who were the buyers? for I feel my fate to be entwined with those water pots. But the merchant replied, saying: Who knows or remembers or cares who buys a water pot, for are these goods sold on credit? Do not the women come and haggle and argue and who wishes to remember these transactions?

So Daoud departed from the coffee-house and his heart was heavy with grief, and he wandered through the streets of Baghdad, thinking: Where is my wealth that I may recover it? And he thought after this fashion: These water pots do not allow the hand to enter, nor do they require cleaning, for they are only used in the closet. Nor can they be used elsewhere, since they have not the graceful curved spout of the ones used for washing hands after food. Therefore she who buys it will not cleanse it. She will merely set it in the closet and fill it with water, and the handkerchief will prevent the gold from chinking or making a noise. Therefore, whoever its owner, the gold is undiscovered. Why should I not go from house to house and gain entry to their closets by a trick, and then in the privacy of the closet I will empty the pots of water and poke in a stick and so discover my gold.

So Daoud returned to the market and he bought a tray of needles and he took them in his hands and he went to a street and he knocked on the door of a house, crying: Needles for sale. And when the door was opened, he said to the slave, the opener: Permit me to use your closet, for I have the gripes. And then in the privacy of the closet he emptied the water pot and poked in his stick, but he did not find his treasure. And then he went to the next house and another house and another house in this manner, and so to the next street, and in the day he visited forty houses.

And the children and small boys who were playing in the houses and streets discussed him, saying: The needle-seller entered our house and entered our closet. And on the next day and for many days and for months Daoud went on visiting houses and entering closets, and the children were aware of this, saying: The Christian needle seller goes to every house and he enters the closet and uses it and empties the water jar. Then he goes to another house and another house and he behaves in this fashion at every house? And the boys asked in the streets: Will the stomach of Daoud never empty? And others would reply: He is even as the camel, for does a camel like its droppings to fall in one place? Will it not scatter them with its tail even as they fall? And the children said: Verily Daoud is as a camel, for he likes not his droppings to fall in one place.

So it came about that as Daoud walked through the streets the boys would run behind him, crying:

Daoud the Camel, Daoud the Camel,
Where will you drop your droppings today?

And the face of Daoud grew black with shame, and he ceased from visiting houses and from visiting closets. And Daoud sat mourning in the house of his friend, his lodging, nor could he go out from it during the hours of daylight, lest the children follow him, chanting rhymes. And he thought after this fashion: I have visited every house and every closet in Battaween and in Karkh, and I have visited half the closets in Bab es Sharji and Karrada. Do so many closets, then, remain in Baghdad? Rather, my chance of finding my gold increases with every house I visit, for should I visit all houses but one, then I know I shall find my wealth in that last house. For how can it be elsewhere?

P

And how can I lift my hand from a task half done? For perhaps I shall find my treasure in the very next closet and in no other. Therefore, I must continue this work, but since the vulgarity of the children does not permit me to do it in the hours of day, then I must go as a thief in the night to inspect these water pots.

So that night when the moon was high in the sky, and the world and the city were asleep, Daoud went out from his lodging and he went to the next house from those houses which yet remained unvisited, and he scaled the high wall and entered the courtyard and he sought the closet. And when he was in the closet he found the lamp and lit it and he poured the water from the water jar. And it so happened that the lady of the house was troubled by a movement of her stomach, even in the middle of the night. So she rose from her bed and went to the closet and she opened the door, and she saw inside a man, and in his hand was the water pot. Then that lady let out a scream and yell which was heard far from Baghdad. It even woke the farmers and the fishermen beyond the town.

And the master of the house and his sons and servants seized their arms and ran out into the courtyard and they found Daoud in the closet and they surrounded him, crying: A thief, a thief. But one of the servants looked at Daoud and inspected his clothes and his shoes and said: Master, this is no thief. Does a thief wear these shoes? Does a thief dress as a merchant? And the master looked and he saw that Daoud was no thief and his anger rose beyond all control, and he said: O pimp, so you know I have beautiful daughters and you come with lustful intent and you hide in the closet. May I ruin your dear ones if you ever do this again. And the master of the house drew his sword and he struck Daoud a blow in the stomach so that the food came forth from within him and the summons of death was ringing in his ears.

Then the youngest of the sons of the house, a boy of fourteen years, looked at Daoud and he said: Father, you have wronged him. This is no lewd fellow, this is only Daoud the Camel, the closet visitor. Perhaps he was seized with a desire for our closet only and not for our sisters. And the master of the house said: I have heard of the fellow. It is said that God has deprived him of his reason, and his madness takes the form of closet visiting, and to harm the mad is evil. But I think that that blow now struck cannot be unstruck.

The master of the house commanded his servants to bring a litter and they lifted Daoud and took him through the streets to the house of the Moslawi Christian, to the lodging of Daoud, and there they left him, and his friend called a surgeon and they brought water and bathed his wound. But the surgeon said: Verily the Angel of Death is expected here. So they brought the Book of the Christians, even the Bible, and commenced reciting verses. Yet the Angel tarried on the road. And Daoud lay on the bed tossing and moaning in fever and in pain. And he kept saying: The water pot, the water pot. I must find the water pot. And his friends did not understand his words, and they discussed the affair after this fashion, saying: A man on his deathbed should call for his wife and his sons and his loved ones. Why does he babble of water pots? And some of them answered, saying: He is mad. Know you he spent the days of his life in closets. But the wife of his friend said to her son: The words of the dying are words of meaning and wisdom and should be respected. Go to our closet and take the water pot which is within it, and which I bought but a few days before the arrival of our friend, and empty it of water and bring it to us.

And the son went to the closet and he emptied the pot of water and he brought it to them, saying: This is the water pot which Daoud used at the dawning of every day, however many other pots he used later in the day. And they took the pot and shook it over Daoud, after the manner in which a toy is shaken over a baby or a madman, saying: Look at the water pot. What a nice water pot. And as they shook it they heard inside it a dull thud, thud, and they brought a stick and poked it in and found something within it, and they brought wire and fish hooks and drew it forth and it was a bundle tied in a handkerchief, wet with water and heavy with gold, but when they turned to acquaint Daoud of the affair they found that his eyes were filmed by death.

BETWEEN TRUTH AND FALSE-

HOOD LIE FOUR FINGERS

IN the days of the Ottomans there was a wealthy merchant in Basra, and in God only is there belief. The name of the merchant was Mahmud, and his wealth exceeded that of all the merchants of Basra. He was rich with exceeding riches, and he had a wife like unto a star, for she was as graceful as the gazelle, her eyes were like spring pools in the desert, her skin was as delicate as rose petals, her breasts were as two ripe peaches towards which the hand desires to stretch, her waist was slender as a young sapling and her thighs were smooth and lovely. And in virtue she was beyond compare, for she was as the golden shelduck, who pairs only with her mate, and dies if she is deprived of him. The name of this girl was Leila, for she was born in the night, and she was in the seventeenth year of her life.

So Mahmud the Merchant had abundance of those things which make for pleasure in this world. Yet he was not happy nor were the great merchants and bankers his friends, for he was a miser greatly given to suspicion and doubt. His trade was a great trade and it was his custom to go to the shroffs and bankers and he would give them bags of Turkish gold, saying: Here are two thousand Hamidiya liras. Give me their equivalent in Indian rupees or in Persian tomans. The great bankers would take the bag and put it with their gold without opening it or counting it, for this was the custom of men of honour. But when they gave a bag to Mahmud, saying: Take these twenty-five thousand rupees, Mahmud would open the bag and count out the rupees one by one, biting each coin to see that it was good. A crowd would collect to watch him, and the people would say: See how Mahmud counts the money. The banker must be a cheat or the merchant would not behave like this.

214

And the bankers became angry with Mahmud, and they said to him: Since how many years are we in this bazaar? Are our names not known names that you treat us as thieves? And Mahmud would reply to them: Verily the proverb says that between true and false lie four fingers, for if you place your right hand on your head, then the distance between your ear and your eye is measured by four fingers, and that which you hear with your ear may be false, but that which you see with your eye is the truth, nor is there any doubt about it. Therefore must I see these silver rupees.

And one of the bankers, named Daoud, a Nazarene, was angered by the manners and customs of Mahmud, and he said to his friends in the market: Verily Mahmud is a heathen. He is not from you the Moslems nor is he from us the Christians that he behaves in this fashion. For in nothing in this world is there belief, save only in One the Creator, and in all else seen or heard there is doubt. Yet we, to transact our business, must believe each other's words and take a risk, for it takes hours to count twenty-five thousand rupees. And if all of us were to behave in this manner, then our day's work would take us a year to complete. Therefore we should teach Mahmud a lesson and give him a warning, if he will profit from a warning, and caution him, if he will listen to a caution, that he is but a son of Adam to whom nothing is certain and nothing is known, save that he is a mortal created by the One God. And the bankers and money changers agreed with the words of Daoud and they said: Verily he shall be taught a teaching.

The next day Mahmud came to the market and he came to the shop of the Nazarene, and he said: Here are ten thousand gold Hamidiya liras. Give me Arabian dollars. And Daoud put the bag with his gold without counting it, and he took four great bags of silver and he gave them to Mahmud, saying: Here are four bags, each containing ten thousand silver dollars of Arabia, and this is your exchange.

Mahmud took the four bags and he opened one of them and he began biting the silver dollars and ringing them on a stone and stacking them in piles of ten that they might be counted the easier, and Daoud the Nazarene sat watching him. And after the first hour the counting of the first bag was still incomplete. Then Daoud spoke and said: Verily your proverb is a true proverb that between truth and falsehood lie four fingers, and unless a man witnesses with his eyes he cannot believe. Yet I think there is one matter in which Your Honour believes for which you lack the evidence of your eyes.

Mahmud replied and said: I believe nothing unless I see it. I count every coin of the money I take. I measure every yard of the cloth I buy. I weigh every bag of corn, of sugar, of rice, and of barley, that enters my warehouse. And I even watch over my warehouse at night, for I do not trust the words of the watchman that he will remain wakeful. Then Daoud asked: But how do you know that your wife Leila is virtuous? Mahmud was angered and he answered: Do you doubt the honour of my house? I want your life, for you reflect also on my honour. Why, Leila's very name is a synonym for virtue in Basra. But Daoud continued, and he asked: Since she is not now before your eyes, how do you know that she is not even at this very moment lying with some lewd fellow?

Mahmud thought and replied: She is virtuous, and was there a way to test her I would surely test her, for this is my custom. But how can one test the honour of a woman?

216

For she is not like a bag of coins that one can count, nor is she like a roll of cloth that one can measure. Then how can the honour of a woman be weighed? Daoud the Nazarene replied and said: There is a way.

Mahmud was interested and he said: Tell me, then, this way, for it is in my mind that I should test the honour of my wife.

Then said Daoud the Nazarene: Write a letter to your wife that you are called away on business to Kuweit, and that you will pass there a fortnight. Send the letter by my shop boy to your wife. Then go to the shop that sells disguises, and return here as a bearded stranger. Then shall I tell you how you can test your wife. And Mahmud wrote the letter, and he left the shop of Daoud the Nazarene to go to the shop of disguises.

And when Mahmud was gone Daoud gave the letter to the shop boy and he said: Deliver this letter to the Mistress Leila, and when you return from her house pluck for me a sweet lime from the tree that grows beneath her window. But let nobody see you take it, and give it to me secretly and in private. And the shop boy left to execute the orders of his master. Then Daoud the Nazarene went to the cloth merchant at the end of the market and he said: Did not the Mistress Leila, wife of his honour the Brother, Mahmud the Merchant, come to your shop and buy red silk, spangled with silver stars, not ten days ago? For though she was veiled, who can mistake the grace of her walk? And I saw her walking back with it, and it is from such cloth that the ladies make petticoat trousers. The cloth merchant replied and said: She came here, and I sold her twenty metres of it, for she liked it much. And Daoud the Christian said: Give me then a snippet of that cloth that I may show it to my wife, for

217

she is pestering me for a present and I am minded to give her some of this cloth. But first I must show it to her and gain her approval, for the man who buys cloth for a woman without her approval is like one who takes a grape and offers it to a hungry tigress. So the merchant cut a snippet from the roll of cloth and gave it to the Christian.

And as Daoud returned to his shop from the cloth merchant, his shop boy returned from the house of Mahmud. Daoud took from him a sweet lime, and he went into his house which stood at the back of his shop, and he caught his she-cat and pulled out one of her whiskers. Then he took a seed pearl and he wrapped it in the snippet of the cloth, and he put it with the cat's whisker and the sweet lime in a handkerchief and he left the parcel in his house.

After a time Mahmud returned from the shop of disguises, and Daoud was amazed, for Mahmud was dressed as a bearded Persian, nor could he be recognised. And Mahmud sat in Daoud's shop, and he said: Now what do I have to do to test my wife? Daoud answered and said: Now send her a message in the code of love. Mahmud asked: What is this code and how do I send a message in it? Daoud asked: Are you, then, such an ignorant lover? Then Daoud called his shop boy and ordered him: Go and bring me a rose, and a phial of crystal glass containing pure clear water, and a moth, and a flask of wine, and a silk handkerchief.

And after half an hour the shop boy returned with all these articles and he laid them in front of his master. Then Daoud took from his treasury a silver Persian toman and he laid the coin on the table with the other articles. Then Daoud the Christian turned to Mahmud the Moslem and he said: Know you that this is the message written in these

218

articles in the universal language of love, as it is spoken in the lands of the Arabs and of the Turks and of the Hindus and of the Franks and of the Chinese, for this language is one understood by lovers and by ladies in every country of the world. Your message reads as follows: You are as delicate and lovely as the petals of a rose. I thirst after you as the gazelle thirsts for pure water. I am drawn to you as the moth is drawn to a candle. You quicken my heart even as wine quickens it and I am a Persian and a stranger.

Then Daoud wrapped up the articles in the silken handkerchief and he said: I will give the packet now to one of my maidservants who is discreet, that she will deliver it to your wife. Then shall we await a reply and then we shall know if she be virtuous or not. And Mahmud said: Do this, that I may know the truth. So Daoud took the packet and he went into his house, but he did not give it to the maidservant, instead he locked it in a cabinet. And he returned and sat in the shop with Mahmud and they discussed business and affairs and passed the time in conversation.

And after two hours Daoud said: I will go and see if the maidservant has returned. And he entered his house and went into his room and he took from it that other packet containing the cat's whisker, the sweet lime, the snippet of cloth and the pearl, and he returned to the shop and gave the packet to Mahmud, saying: This is the reply.

Mahmud opened the packet and he was amazed. He said: What mean these things? This sweet lime is like those on the trees outside my window. This cloth is from my wife's petticoat trousers. But what is this whisker? Daoud looked at the articles and he said: Let me interpret this message, for you are unskilled in this language. This whisker is the whisker of a cat, and its meaning is: Come secretly like a cat in the night. The sweet lime from your tree means: Climb up the tree to my window. And as for this piece of cloth, it is wrapped up and there is something inside it. And Daoud opened the snippet of cloth and he said: Its meaning is this: When you remove my petticoat trousers you shall find a pearl.

Mahmud was seized with fury and his face went black with rage. He put his hand on his dagger and shouted: I shall go now to kill this prostitute and cleanse my honour. But Daoud said: Stay, you must see your wife's dishonour with your own eyes. Else you cannot believe in it. You are now dressed as a Persian and you cannot be recognised. Go unto your wife in the night, and climb the tree and enter her window, then if you are able to take off her petticoat trousers and she screams not to rouse the servants, then shall you know that she is dishonourable. And Mahmud said: Have I not seen enough in this message? But Daoud answered: Perhaps she means to trick a lewd fellow to teach him a lesson. You must be sure before you kill your wife.

So Mahmud controlled himself and he sat to await the coming of night. But as for Daoud the Nazarene, he slipped away and told the other bankers the story of those events known to you, my listeners, and they laughed until the breath was gone from their lungs, and they asked Daoud: But what will happen at Mahmud's house to-night? And Daoud replied: He will climb up the sweet lime tree and enter her window, but before he can take off her petticoat trousers she will scream for the servants. They will come and give him a beating for they will think him a stranger, and this will be his lesson. And it will be one difficult to forget, for he is too much of a yokel to invent

a story for his wife. So he will tell her the truth, she will be greatly angered, and in after years, whenever they quarrel, she will recall these events to him, nor will he ever be allowed to forget them. And the bankers said: O Daoud, you have indeed prepared a fine lesson for our brother in commerce.

Mahmud the Merchant sat in the shop biting his finger-nails from very impatience until the sun set and the moon rose, and the people of the town barred their doors and went to their beds and the town fell asleep.

Then when the town was quiet he gripped the hilt of his dagger and strode towards his house, thinking: Now my eyes shall witness the truth. And he came to his house and all was quiet. So he climbed up the sweet lime tree towards the balcony of his wife's room. And he was a great and heavy merchant, nor had he climbed a tree since his boyhood. So he puffed and panted as he pulled himself up with difficulty, and he put out his right hand and grasped the balcony above him. Yet he had not the strength to pull himself up. So he shoved with his legs upon the branch beneath him that he might be thrust upwards, and such was the strength of his shove that the branch splintered and fell away, and he was left hanging by his right arm with the fingers of his right hand grasping the balcony and his thumb beneath it.

And his wife Leila heard the crack of the branch and she came out. Yet she was not of the screaming, fainting women. She was a true Arab and she came out with a scimitar in her hand, and when she saw the fingers of a man grasping the balcony she cut at them and she severed those four fingers from his hand with one blow, and he fell to the ground. Then Leila called to the servants and they came out with sticks and started beating the man on the ground, but Mahmud pulled off his beard and discovered himself to them. Then Leila questioned Mahmud as to the reason for the masquerade as she bandaged the stumps of his fingers, and since he was unskilled in the art of love, he told her the truth, and she spoke to him, and her words were words of bitter scorn.

And in the morning Mahmud went to the market-place to change money, and the merchants saw that his right hand was bandaged and that it had no fingers. And when Mahmud took the bags of money from the bankers, he did not open them nor did he count the money. He accepted their word. And when they questioned him concerning the loss of his fingers he did not reply to them. And when he was gone the bankers gathered together and said: It was our intention to teach a lesson, and verily a lesson has been taught. Yet it went beyond our teaching. And in after years whenever Mahmud argued or questioned the words of a man of Basra, those present would remark: Between true and false lie four fingers. And Mahmud would become silent and walk away.

THE STORY OF ABDUL

REHMAN ABU SULTAN AND
THE TONGUE OF THE DEAD

WHAT do you know of El Iraq, you who are boys? I was an old man before the First German War, and I know the country and its history, yet you say there is no monster in the Hor el Hammar. I have seen it, thirty years ago, for this monster takes on the shape of a woman, and it beckons to a man that he may enter the lake, and every twelve years it must eat a man. I have seen it beckoning on the edge of the lake on the nights when there was no moon, but I did not follow it, for I knew its history, and I know that a man must carry a needle when away from his house at night, yet you know nothing of these things, and you are like Abdul Rehman Abu Sultan, who was so ignorant that he desired nothing but money, and who was so foolish that he tried to rob the dead without listening to warnings or heeding cautions that the sons of Adam shall not meddle with magic and strange matters, nor shall they interfere with those that live beyond the end of the world, nor shall they disturb those that await the Last Day.

Abdul Rehman Abu Sultan was a carpenter of Basra, and he lived in his house with a young and lovely wife and with a fine son, yet he was not happy, for his earnings were few and his house was a poor house of bowari matting and his food was but dates and bread. And winter came and the rains fell and everything in Abdul Rehman's house was wet, even to the blankets of his bed, for the matting did not keep out the rain, and the cold wind whistled through the walls of his house, and he was in a miserable and desperate state, so he went to the coffee-house to get warm and he met there his friends, and he discussed his condition, saying: How can I get money to buy a dry house, and a sheep for the feast and clothes for my wife? And they replied, and said: Did we but know a way would we be sitting here? A man must work and earn a little money for the needs of his house, and this is man's fate in this world that he must work and yet be poor. Ours is a life of striving and endeavour, and wealth will come to us when God wills and at no other time. But one of the men who was sitting in the coffee-house said: There is a way to get rich that will give you so much gold that you cannot carry it and so many rare jewels that you cannot count them and so much knowledge that you will be master of the world, and this in the course of a single day. And Abdul Rehman asked: If you know this way, then why do you labour? And the man said: I know the way to get rich, but I like it not, for it is to rob the dead. And those that were there present lifted their hands and said: We take refuge in God from this conduct. But Abdul Rehman said: If you know of gold that belongs to the dead, tell me where it is, that I may acquire it, for what need have the dead of gold?

And the man replied and said: I was wandering around the ruined city of Tell el Ummgaya, and when I had reached the edge of the city which is towards the desert to the west, it so happened that I was tired and I sat down by a mound and I pulled from my pocket the box in which I carry cigarette paper and tobacco, for I wanted to smoke. And I tried to open the box, but it was tight, and when from the force of my fingers the lid flew open the contents were also thrown out, and in that box I had placed a silver dirhem, and the coin fell to the ground and rolled down the slope and entered a hole in the ground. And since I had no other money with me I was forced to pursue that dirhem, and I found that the hole into which it had fallen was large enough for me to enter, yet I was unwilling to do so, for it was dim and black within. But

226

I do not lack courage, and there was no money with me for my supper, so I entered the hole and descended. I struck a match to find the dirhem. And by the light of that match I saw the dirhem and I also saw that a great passage led away from the hole under the ground. And I picked up my dirhem from the ground and I was in mind to see where the passage went, so I lit other matches and went down the passage, and in this manner I travelled for a great distance under the very surface of the earth, until I came to a great door, studded with iron and with brass, and on it I saw by the light of a match writing in Arabic which read: Let the seeker who seeks kiss this door, then shall he enter. And though it was in my thoughts that lawful and honest matters do not hide from the light of the sun beneath the ground in dark caverns, yet I could not turn back without opening that door, so I tried it with my hand, but it did not yield, nor could I find any key-hole or bolt. So I placed my lips to that door and kissed it, and even as I kissed it I felt it move backwards and swing open and I found before me a chamber and along each wall hung skeletons of men, and on the ground were the bones of the dead, and in the middle of the chamber was a great pile of gold and jewels and rare stones, and on the pile was seated a great and full woman, yet on her body there was not cloth nor was there covering, her flesh was alive and ample, and her lips were the colour of blood. And I asked of her and demanded: Who be you and what do you in this evil place? And she answered and said: I am she who will make you richer than Solomon the King, and I shall give you so much gold that you cannot carry it, and so many rare jewels that you cannot count them, and so much knowledge that you will be master of the world, and all I ask of you is that you take me in your arms and kiss my lips, then shall you say these words: I accept your lips and I accept your body and I accept your tongue. Then shall you pass your tongue through my lips into my mouth and I shall press my tongue through your lips into your mouth, and I shall reveal to you miracles of knowledge and of wealth. And I said to her: This thing will I do, but first shall you say the creed, that I may know if you be good or evil. And she replied and said: Those words my tongue shall not utter. Then verily I knew her to be evil and I turned from her and fled, nor did I stop running until I came to the outer world and the heat of the sun, in which evil and horrible things cannot linger.

And Abdul Rehman Abu Sultan heard the words of his friend, and he said: You were lacking in courage and enterprise, for if a man be truly brave he fears nothing in the World or in Land of Doom, and if you show me the cavern in which this woman sits then I shall unseat her from her pile of gold, and I will make her think of other things than tongues before I leave her, and when I go I will take with me her treasure, for I have no fear. And those that were present in the coffee-house drew up their cloaks from the ground and said: There is no strength nor power save in God, and we take refuge in God from one so evil that he would meddle in these affairs. But the friend of Abdul Rehman said: If you will not listen to wisdom and if you mock those who heed warnings and who abstain from evil things, then I will show you the entrance to this cavern, but I will not accompany you nor will I help you, nor shall you again enter my house nor will I sit with you again in a coffee-house, for verily your companions shall be the jackals and hyenas who dig at the graves at night.

But Abdul Rehman was wet and cold and his stomach

was empty of meat and good food, so he said: You shall show me the place.

So on the morning of the next day Abdul Rehman and his friend took camels and they left Basra, and their destination was Tell el Ummgaya. And after three days spent on the road they saw before them the hill and the time was evening and the sun was in the west. And Abdul Rehman said to his friend: Guide me to the hole in the ground and to the passage and to the door. And his friend replied: Would you then enter when it is night over the world? And Abdul Rehman said: I have no fear. So Abdul Rehman was guided by his friend to that part of the ruins and former dwellings of ancient men which lies towards the desert to the west, and his friend pointed with his finger to a hole in the ground saying: Here shall you enter, and strange and extraordinary matters lie ahead of you, but as for me, I shall march for Basra this very night, nor shall I again speak to you or hear your voice or see your face. And his friend and companion of the road turned and mounted his camel and departed from him, and Abdul Rehman was left without any of the sons of Adam near him, for around him were only the dwellings of the dead and of the wild and savage beasts of the desert.

And Abdul Rehman entered the hole and he entered the dark passage which lay under the surface of the earth, and it was cold and damp within and there was a smell of slimy and evil things and there was the smell of the dead. And Abdul Rehman sat down on the ground and there was fear in his heart and he thought: Why must I desire wealth and money and power, for if a man has all the wealth in the world, his stomach can only hold the food of one man, nor can he eat more, nor are the girls that he can love unlimited. When I go to my home after a day of

230

labour the food tastes good to me, though it be cheap. Does, then, the richest merchant in the city enjoy his quails and duck and partridges more than I enjoy my bread and dates? And can man be happier than I with my wife, for if there be not love what pleasure has a man in a woman? Truly the rich men with their great and fat bellies are no happier than I, for we are the same as they are, and what wealth or power does a man have when his eyes grow dim and his legs grow weak and his hand quivers and his voice grows faint, and the worms and the insects of the earth will eat their bodies even as they will eat my body? And it was in Abdul Rehman's thoughts that he should return back and abandon his purpose, but he thought: Those words which I spoke in the coffee-house will be remembered against me, and men will say to me: You mocked us and boasted of your courage, yet you are less than we, who know that we are but created beings and withdraw our hands from evil and forbidden matters.

So Abdul Rehman continued on under the surface of the earth until he came to the great door, and though his hand was shaking and his stomach sick with fear he pressed his lips to the door and said: Open. And the door swung open and he saw within a chamber lit with a green light, and along each wall hung skeletons of men and on the ground were the bones of the dead and in the middle of the chamber was a great pile of gold and jewels and rare stones and on the pile was seated a great and full woman, yet on her body there was not cloth nor was there covering: her flesh was alive and ample and her lips were the colour of blood. And Abdul Rehman demanded of her: Who be you and what do you here? And she replied saying: I am she who will make you richer than Solomon the King, and I shall give you so much gold that you cannot carry it and so many rare jewels that you cannot count them and so much knowledge that you will be master of the world, and all I ask of you is that you take me in your arms and kiss my lips, then shall you say these words: I accept your lips and I accept your body and I accept your tongue. Then shall you pass your tongue through my lips into my mouth and I shall press my tongue through your lips into your mouth and I shall reveal to you miracles of knowledge and of wealth. And it was in Abdul Rehman's thought that he turn back for he was faint with fear, but he thought: My friends will mock me. So he took the woman in his arms and kissed her on the lips and he said the words: I accept your lips and I accept your body and I accept your tongue. Then Abdul Rehman put his lips to her lips and he pressed with his tongue against her lips and her lips parted and the tip of his tongue entered her mouth. Then Abdul Rehman shook with very fear and he tried to escape and leave the woman, for he found that his tongue was drawn and sucked into her mouth by a great force, nor could he stop it or control it, nor could he tear himself away from the woman, for the strength was gone from his limbs. And it happened that the tongue of Abdul Rehman was pulled away from its roots and it vanished completely into the mouth of the woman and there was a gush of blood in his mouth. Then again the woman pressed her lips to his lips and the tip of her tongue entered his mouth and he shuddered and trembled, for the feel of her tongue was as is the skin of a dead snake. Then her tongue entered his mouth, nor could he stop it, nor could his lips prevent it, and only when her tongue had fully entered his mouth was he able to move and escape, for then the flesh fell from her bones and her eyes fell out and she fell

232

to the ground, a withered skeleton. But her tongue lay in his mouth and it was cold and horrible, and his fingers could not pluck it out. And he tried to say the holy words which avert evil things and banish them, but the words did not come, for the tongue was not his tongue. Then the tongue spoke and though the words came from his mouth he did not know the words until he heard them with his ears, for they were not his words. And the tongue said: Know you that I am the Tongue of the Dead, and though I shall keep my promise to you, and give you so much gold that you cannot carry it and so many rare jewels that you cannot count them, and so much knowledge that you shall be master of the world, yet in all else you must obey me, and when I say turn to the left you shall turn to the left and when I say turn to the right you shall turn to the right, for though you master the world I am your master. And the tears streamed from Abdul Rehman's eyes, though no sob or sound came from his mouth.

And the Tongue commanded him that he march for Basra, so he left that chamber and came out from under the earth and the world was night. And he found his camel and mounted and set out on the road. And he was three days on the road and he ate of dates and cheese, yet he could not taste the food and it was without flavour. And on the evening of the third day he came to Basra and he went towards his house. And as he passed the coffee-house men came out, saying: Abdul Rehman has returned. And one of the men cried out to him, mocking: Abdul Rehman Abu Sultan, where is your bag of gold? But the Tongue replied, saying: Do you mock me, you whom all should mock. He who is at your side lay with your wife last night, and if you want proof of it, does not the great bed in your house lie against the wall and is not the wall covered with red plaster, and who else has this plaster in their house? Look, then, at your friend's left arm and shoulder, for has it not been rubbing against that plaster. And the man looked and saw that it was true, so he drew his knife and leapt at the man, crying: A death to cleanse an injury. But the other man also drew his knife and before they could be restrained both were lying on the ground, one with his stomach ripped open and the other with his throat dashed open and the blood of their lives was flowing away. And the Tongue said to Abdul Rehman: Can any mock the Master of the World? But Abdul Rehman thought: They were my friends. And Abdul Rehman came to his house, and his loved wife, his girl Aina, came out to welcome him and she cried: Thanks be to God for your safe return; your presence is a present of happiness. But the Tongue cried out: Come, neighbours. Come, witnesses. And all who heard were astonished. Then in a great voice the Tongue commenced saying the Oath of Divorce, and the girl Aina burst out sobbing and weeping, but those present said: She is better gone from him, for see, he is like a madman; though the words come clearly from his mouth, it is as if his hands were trying to stop them and his face is a face of horror and disgust. And when the divorce was completed and the girl Aina had gone weeping away Abdul Rehman entered his house and he saw there his boy Sultan, a fine boy in the tenth year of his age, and the boy was weeping, for he had heard the words of Divorce. And Abdul Rehman tried to speak to his son and excuse himself, but no words came; instead the Tongue spoke, saying: O my son, I test your obedience. Climb on to the wooden shaft above the well. And the boy was obedient, and he climbed up and stood on the shaft. But Abdul Rehman thought:

234

The Tongue means evil. So he ran towards the boy to protect him from evil and to take him in his arms. But as he ran the Tongue let out a dreadful cry, full of evil and fear, and when the boy Sultan saw his father running towards him crying a dreadful cry, he became afraid, so he turned away, but the shaft was narrow and he slipped and fell to the bottom of the well, and since the well was dry his backbone snapped, and Abdul Rehman was overcome with grief at the death of his son nor did he desire wealth nor did he desire to become master of the world, his one thought was to be free of the Tongue. So he left his house and went to the city and he tried to enter a mosque, but whenever he came near the door of a holy place the Tongue curled in his throat so that he choked, nor could he breathe the air. And it happened that he was walking on the bank of the river when he came on a derwish, an old man frail and white of beard. And he cast himself at the feet of the derwish and he wrote in the dust the letters: Say over me La hol. And though the Tongue choked him nearly to death, he wrote the words and the derwish read them and was astonished, and he said the verse. And when it heard the holy words the Tongue shook and such was the force of its shaking that Abdul Rehman was forced back into the river, but the Tongue came out of his mouth and it swam away like a great leech. Then up came four great fish, each six paces long and black of skin, and each fish seized a limb of Abdul Rehman and tore it off, and he was left without arms or legs. And slowly the derwish, who was frail and old, pulled Abdul Rehman from the river, and he had no limbs. And the fish vanished, nor did they touch the derwish. And men came and they carried Abdul Rehman to a surgeon, and he bound his stumps, but when they questioned him he did not reply and they saw that he had no tongue. And they looked in his eyes and they saw that his reason was gone from him, for his eyes had the dim look of a mad dog. So when his stumps were healed they set him in a doorway, that those that passed and the charitable and the merciful might lift a little water and food to his lips. And the wealthy and generous threw at him coins, sometimes gold and sometimes jewels and they lay on the ledge beside him, nor could he pick them up, nor did any steal them, for who would rob a man with no hands and no legs.

And it happened that a wise man of the Arabs was passing through Basra in the company of the learned, and he was astonished at his condition, and he ordered that there be written above Abdul Rehman the words: Here is he who has so much gold that he cannot carry it and so many rare jewels that he cannot count them and so much knowledge that he is master of the world. And to those who questioned him he said: How much gold can a man carry with no legs and no arms, and how many jewels can a man count with no fingers, and the mad are masters of the world, for they are not bound by that which binds us, nor are they worried by cravings and desires, and the fountain of knowledge is the fear of God.

NOTES

1. THE STORY OF HAJJI ALI, THE GREAT SULTAN AND HIS SON, THE AMIR KHEYYUN

The Maadan. Page 12, Line 17. 'The Maadan shall bring milk.'

The Maadan are in the main a tribe of poor families, living in scattered communities on the shores of that great area of marsh and lake which lies between the Tigris and the Euphrates before the two rivers finally join to form the Shatt el Arab. Maadan villages often acknowledge the authority of sheikhs of neighbouring tribes, and they have no great tradition of their own. Their chief source of wealth was in the past their large herds of water buffaloes, their income being derived from the sale of milk and its products, lebn (a kind of curd), and clarified cooking butter. The sale of milk is regarded as shameful by most tribes, though of course all produce enough for their own requirements. In consequence the Maadan, with their trade in milk and hides, are looked down on by the tribes, and they are said to be lacking in honour. However in the last twenty-five years the Maadan have acquired large areas of agricultural land, and they are sharing fully in the increasing wealth of South Iraq. As for their honour, I remember a fight three years ago which took place between two Maadan subsections not far from Qarmat Ali, just outside Basra. This was a fight for a woman's honour in the best tribal tradition in which nothing was lacking either in the number of rounds of ammunition expended or in the casualties to bring it fully up to the standard of the great tribes in these matters.

2. A STORY CONCERNING THE IGNORANCE OF SLAVES

Slaves.

'Abd, or slave, is a slang expression in South Iraq for a Negro, and does not now indicate an actual slave. Slavery continued in Iraq to the end of Ottoman rule, 83 years after its abolition in the British Empire. In this story, therefore, the word would refer to actual slaves, and I have so translated it. The word 'habshi' (lit. 'Abyssinian') is little used in South Iraq, a Negro being referred to as a 'sambo' or 'abd'.

Crocodile. Page 20, Line 3. 'In that river was a crocodile.'

The word used was 'timsah', or crocodile, of which of course there are none in Iraq. I do not know if this indicates that this story

238

originates from Africa, possibly as one told by Negroes themselves. There are sharks in the Shatt el Arab and in the Karun River in Arabistan which occasionally take off the leg of a bather as far as eighty miles from the sea and the shark is far better known to the Iraqi than is the crocodile.

4. The Story of the Prince of Kermanshah and of His Misfortunes

Peacock. Page 29, Line 25. 'A thousand peacocks.'

I think this bird is only included to give an exotic flavour to the feast. I remember once mentioning that I had shot and eaten peafowl in the Punjab, a statement which was received with much surprise and, I am afraid, some lack of belief, and on a subsequent occasion when someone was describing a feast one of those present shouted, 'Put in a peacock for the Sahib'. In India the peacock is not normally killed by Moslems on the grounds that it is a bird of Paradise. In Iraq, however, I do not doubt that the learned doctors of religion could give the answer straight away if asked. Pigeons which roost on mosques are exempt from molestation, even when destroying crops outside villages. There is incidentally a pretty Iraqi story which explains the large feet of a pigeon. It describes how the pride and arrogance of peacocks offended King Solomon, so to punish them he took away their feet and gave them the feet of the pigeons, that they might always be shamed by their smallness, while the peacocks' large and beautiful feet he gave of course to the pigeons.

5. The Story of the Youth Jamil, the Son of a Merchant in Baghdad

Page 43, Line 3. 'The City of Peace.'

Medinat es Salaam or 'City of Peace' is one of the names used in poetry for Baghdad. The city, when first built, was originally named Medinat es Salaam, but it appears that people persisted in referring to it as Baghdad, or Dad's Garden, from some older name for the site of the present city. Arabs love these poetical names, differing from those in normal use. Iraq is sometimes known as Bilad er Rafidain, or Country of the Two Rivers, Jerusalem (Al Quds or the Holy in

Arabic) is sometimes known as Bet al Maqadas, or the Holy House.
Cousin. Page 44, Line 13. 'Has she a cousin?'

The right of a man to ask for his cousin in marriage is still maintained in the tribes. Should the girl or her parents not desire the marriage it may be necessary in some cases to compensate the man for the loss of his right. Family opinion is also a powerful factor tending to force a man to marry his cousin. In spite of all this, however, the bulk of marriages are between different families, and a surprisingly large number of marriages would appear to be between different tribes. The railway is increasing this tendency, as a man gets employment away from home and frequently marries a girl in the area in which he is working. I remember meeting tribesmen driving lorries in Persia who expressed the desire to take back a Persian wife, but who were anxious about the reception she might meet at their homes. I am told that some did in fact do so, concealing the girls on their lorries when crossing the frontier at Khaniqin.

6. The Story of the Lost Soul

Page 60, Line 17. 'A caravan from Persia carrying bodies for burial.'

The majority of Persians are of the Shia section of Islam, so wealthy families send their dead to Iraq for burial. The usual custom is for families to come on pilgrimage to the cities of Kerbala, Nejf, and Kadhimain, and to bring the body for burial at the same time. This is many months after the time of death, for Iraqi health regulations now ban the import of recently dead corpses. The body is therefore buried in Persia near to the place of death and dug up when in condition to travel. It is no uncommon thing in a Persian graveyard to see a wooden stretcher lying on top of a tomb to indicate that the family intend to send the body for burial in holier soil, though it appears that poverty or forgetfulness after the passage of months often interfere with the actual journey. However, the sight of Persian pilgrims putting a coffin on to the train at Maqil Railway Station is not an uncommon one. Should the family themselves not be able to travel they might have to rely on agents, but it would be the duty of the dead man's eldest son to go with the body if unavoidable circumstances, such as military service or the lack of a passport, did not make it impossible.

Arab time. Page 63, Line 32. 'And the time was the sixth hour of night.'

Arab time has long since been abandoned in Iraq though it continues in modified forms in the Persian Gulf and elsewhere. The Arab day of the week or date starts at sunset (e.g. the Arab Monday would start at sunset on our Sunday). The first twelve hours of each day of the week, that is, from sunset to twelve hours later, were known as the Hours of Night. They were followed by twelve further hours known as the Hours of Day, to complete the 24 hour cycle and to make one complete day. The sixth hour of night would thus be six hours after sunset, probably somewhere near our midnight. The Arab time system had many disadvantages, but probably for people living in the desert without watches, and therefore forced to use the sun or stars to tell them the time, it was as good a system as any. Sunset was the same for everybody and started the day, sunrise would in practice in the desert be considered to be twelve hours later and therefore the start of the first hour of day. Noon was, under the same casual reckoning, the sixth hour of day. In practice Arabs are extremely good at judging the time from noting the passage of the moon or stars, though I suppose that they will in time lose this gift through the present almost universal possession of watches.

7. THE STORY OF MAQDAD—HE WAS THE HERO OF HILLA

Hilla.

Hilla is an old Arab town situated at a crossing of the Euphrates River near to the ancient site of Babylon. Al Fetla have of course no special claim to the town and I was surprised that Maqdad should be hero of Hilla rather than of one of the smaller places to which Al Fetla could lay a closer claim. I think one tends to forget that many of the smaller towns and villages were insignificant or did not exist at all until recent times. Nasiriya, for example, which the Muntafiq tribes now regard as their capital, and which is the seat of the Mutassarif of the Muntafiq Liwa, was only founded in the last century by Nasir Pasha es Saadun. Hilla must in the past have been the centre of a very much larger area than it is today. It is still one of the most important towns of South Iraq. It is well known beyond the borders of Iraq as being mentioned in a nursery rhyme which runs:

Cukukhti, wein ukhti?	Dove, where's my sister?
B'il Hilla.	In Hilla.
Sha takal?	What does she eat?
Bajilla.	Beans.
Wein tenam?	Where does she sleep?
Bab Illah	At God's door.

and which continues for several verses.

The mace. Page 71, Line 16. 'A mace of the finest teakwood.'

The mace may almost be said to be a traditional weapon in South Iraq. If you meet an Arab tribesman about his normal daily routine in the countryside, he will probably be armed with a mace and dagger. Rifles are weapons of luxury, to be kept away from dust and damp. Many tribal dances are done with the mace, which is sometimes of solid wood carefully carved, and sometimes, a less beautiful weapon but more dangerous, it is made of a wooden shaft with a ball of lead or pitch at the end.

Page 74, Line 22. 'Maqdad took his course from the wind.'

Skilled desert guides can often recognise a wind as being from a certain quarter by its force, humidity, and temperature. The phrase here implies that the sun was clouded over and Maqdad was finding his way by the wind, which indicates that he had considerable skill. The only people who can use the wind are those who can detect quickly any change in its direction. I remember once asking some Arabs the way to a well, and they told me, Keep the wind on your left cheek. I had to use methods with which I was more familiar.

Page 81, Line 25. 'Now I shall call myself Ibn Ali.'

The kunya, or name defining a person by his relationship to some-one else, is recorded both in classical and modern Arabic usage. Ibn Batuta, for example, a famous fourteenth century traveller, is known only by his kunya. The modern tribal practice appears to be to promote a man to a kunya when he becomes the father of a boy. A man who has become father of a boy named Qais will, for example, be hailed by his friends with exceptional heartiness for some weeks afterwards, 'Ahlan wa sahlan ya Ab Qais', and the name may or may not stick to him permanently. Women are almost invariably known by the name of their eldest son, preceded of course by Umm. The other extremely common practice is that of giving a man a laqab, or nickname, from some habit or personal peculiarity. The laqab is rarely complimentary.

8. A Man's Honour is in the Hair of His Moustache

Page 111, Line 14. 'The hub in their house was empty of water.'

The hub is a large porous earthenware jar, which keeps water cool by evaporation.

Page 112, Line 6. 'Nor did he even own the leg of a mare.'

The phrase 'leg of a mare' implies that a man has ownership in a quarter share of the sale price of all foals from the mare. It is quite common for deals to be done in one, two, or three legs of a mare, and for one mare to have four owners.

Page 116, Line 13. 'Then will our sheikh cry, Sheil.'

Sheil, or Take away, is a word commonly used as an order to strike camp.

Page 116, Line 28. 'You should not have to drink the water from a camel's stomach.'

When threatened by death from thirst in the desert, Arabs may be forced to slaughter their camels in order to drink the stomach fluids. I have also been told that travellers have made their camels sick by forcing a stick down their throats to get a little fluid. I do not know if this is true. It would appear to me to be a most difficult operation.

Page 118, Line 29. 'Cut my head to keep the secret.'

This should probably have been more properly translated 'Cut my head off to keep the secret,' for I have since been told one man's version of this saying. According to his account there were three brothers of a famous Nejaf family, living in poverty, and they were forced to become thieves. One day they went to raid a Turkish Army camp near to Hindya. In the daytime they watched the camp and saw which was the guard tent in which the treasure chest was hidden. They then waited till night, and, when the camp was asleep, they crept up to the guard tent. One of the brothers slit the tent wall with his knife and crept inside. Inside the tent he found a box of silver dollars, and he was passing it out through the slit in the tent to his two brothers when he trod on one of the Turks, who woke up and grabbed him by the legs. The Turk was shouting to raise the alarm, and the Nejafi, seeing that he could not get away, and fearing that if he was identified, his whole family would be punished, put his head out through the slit in the tent and implored his brothers to cut it off and take it away. This, according to the story, they did, getting away both with the chest of silver and their brother's head, the identity of the family remaining undiscovered. The word for 'cut' in Arabic does imply cutting off and removing when applied to heads.

10. The Story of the Son of the Pilgrim

Page 148, Line 7. 'He is one of the Shammar princes from Hail.'

The Shammar are mentioned in other stories and a reader may be confused by the different areas from which they appear to come. To write a note on this extensive tribe would require considerable knowledge both of Syria and of Saoudi Arabia, and I myself cannot do it. The Shammar best known to the Muntafiq tribes are the Shammar of Nejd, who send caravans legally to Zobeir, and with less authority to other areas. Some of the Nejdi Shammar do graze in Iraqi territory and in the Neutral Zones. However, the most famous Shammar of Iraq are those of Mosul Liwa. There are also Shammar, some of whom have adopted the Shia religion, living in Baghdad Liwa. Many of them have entered Iraq as refugees after defeat by Ibn Saoud. When a prince of the Shammar from Hail is mentioned, I should think that a member of the Rashid family is indicated. This family were once rulers in Nejd, and their capital was for a time at Hail. They were finally defeated by the Wahabis under Ibn Saoud. The word Amir which I have here translated as prince, is a somewhat deceptive one. The sons of an Arab king carry, it is true, the title of Amir, but the word has a larger usage. The tribes of Northern Arabia and Syria use it in their sheikhly houses, and in the Persian Gulf the word implies little more than a minor local official. The root of Amir is from the Arabic word for 'command' and is most literally translated in such phrases as 'Amir ul Mouminin', that is, 'The Commander of the Faithful".

12. THE STORY OF THE TWO DANCERS

Page 171, Line 1. 'Which was full of chests of Kuweit of enormous size.'

The Kuweit chest is sometimes to be seen in English houses, its owners ignorant of its history. It is normally of polished or carved teakwood studded with brass, and with massive brass hinges and locks which are engraved by hand. In size it may be from four to six feet long, two and a half or three feet high, and of course broad in proportion. It sometimes has a false bottom or secret drawer. I have often hoped that some resident of Kuweit would write a book on these interesting chests. I have seen many of them, beautifully worked, in the bazaars of Baghdad and Basra. I also used to see them when going on board Kuweiti jalbuts from India when they called at Bahrein. There were usually a number of these chests carried as deck cargo, though not as large nor of such good wood as the old ones found in the bazaars. The nakhodas of the craft whom I questioned about these chests informed me that their sailors, in addition to receiving pay, had the right to bring one chest each from India, full of goods to be sold on their own account. I did in fact look through some of these chests and found them in the main stocked with Indian sandals, mirrors, scent, rolls of cloth, saris and similar articles. I was told that in the past Kuweiti sailors would buy the chest in India, stock it with goods, and carve it and put in the heavy brass studs on the voyage back to Kuweit, which might take several months, as the dhows call at a number of small Indian and Persian ports. On arrival at Kuweit or Basra the chests and their contents would be sold, and the price of a well worked chest was an important part of a sailor's earnings. I asked them why the chests on the deck of most of the dhows were without ornament, and was told that at present there was less profit in the sale of the chest than in the goods it contained, and that chests now available in Southern Indian ports were of such poor quality that they did not repay work. They still buy these chests as the sailor's own property is carried as deck cargo, and the goods would be liable to damage by rain or spray if otherwise packed.

13. The Story of Sheikh Mizeil el Qurnachi, a Man of a Noble Family, though His Land Was Poor

Page 185, Line 15. 'and ordered fifty mithkals of them.'
The mithkal is a small weight used by goldsmiths.

Page 188, Line 20. 'Take soldiers and go to Qasr Qurnachi.'
Qasr—castle. 'Qurnachi Castle.'

Page 191, Line 11. 'Can then the hawk fly without wings.'
I was told that this quotation was from a famous Arab poet, but regret that I was unable to place it, and nobody could remember the name of the poet. The quotation as put into the mouth of Sheikh Aqab is particularly apt, as Aqab, though its literal translation is 'eagle,' is a name often given to hawks.

Page 198, Line 24. 'She was clad in an ataq and bag trousers.'
The ataq is a kind of blouse.

14. The Story of Daoud the Camel and of his Misfortunes

Page 204, Line 4. 'The Shammar of the Jezira.'
The area in Mosul Liwa which lies to the west of the Tigris, that is, between the Tigris and the Euphrates, is known as the Jezira, or Island. The Shammar in this area are the famous tribe of the late Sheikh Ajil el Yawar.

15. Between Truth and Falsehood Lie Four Fingers

Page 214, Line 14. 'The name of this girl was Leila for she was born in the night.'
Leila, 'Night,' is a popular girl's name in South Iraq. I do not think it is restricted only to those girls born at night.